What Is Meditation?

JOHN WHITE is director of education at The Institute of Noetic Sciences in Palo Alto, California. The institute was founded in 1973 by Apollo 14 astronaut Edgar D. Mitchell and dedicated to consciousness research and education for solutions to planetary problems. Mr. White is also editor of *The Highest State of Consciousness, Frontiers of Consciousness,* and *Psychic Exploration.* From 1972–73 he was Eastern Editor of *Psychic* magazine. He is presently an associate editor of *Psychic* and an editorial board member of *Journal of Altered States of Consciousness.*

What Is Meditation?

Edited by John White

ANCHOR BOOKS
ANCHOR PRESS/DOUBLEDAY
GARDEN CITY, NEW YORK

The Anchor Books edition is the first publication of *What Is Meditation?*
Anchor Books edition: 1974

ISBN: 0-385-07638-x
Library of Congress Catalog Card Number 73–81126

To A.L.P. AND H.C.E.

Hiara pirlu resh kavawn
J. R. Salamanca, LILITH

Acknowledgments

WHILE PREPARING THIS BOOK, I was guided by four people who freely gave their time and knowledge. They are Beverly Timmons, of Langley Porter Neuropsychiatric Institute in San Francisco, an active meditation researcher; Frank C. Tribbe, of Washington, D.C., a director of Spiritual Frontiers Fellowship; Durand Kiefer, an independent researcher in meditation and higher states of consciousness; and Eric Rathbun, a journeying soul nearing his last incarnation. Without their assistance this book could not have been completed. I acknowledge my debt and gratitude to them.

THE EDITOR

Contents

Introduction

THIS IS AN AGE OF MENTAL EXPLORATION. Partly because of the uncertainty and turbulence of modern times, people are searching for answers to the big questions in life—answers that have traditionally been given by established institutions of society but that no longer seem sufficient. Meditation is one of the areas to which people are turning in their search for understanding and certainty.

Meditation is a means of growth, both personal and transpersonal. This will never be a better world until there are better people in it, and meditators claim that the best way—indeed, the only way—for people to change is by "working on yourself" from within, through meditation.

The highest goal of meditation is enlightenment. Spiritual teachers of all ages have been unanimous in declaring that we can come to know God through meditation. Through direct experience—not through bookish learning or intellectual conceptualization—we may reach a state of conscious union with the ultimate reality and divine dimension of the universe. In that state all the long-sought answers are given, along with peace of mind and heart. There are other paths to God-knowledge, of course, but this is one path easily available to many and the chief reason for the world-wide interest and enduring value placed on meditation.

By meditating, a person can improve himself physically, psychologically, and socially. Physical illnesses and ailments are usually improved and sometimes even cured. (A U. S. Air Force physician recently reported healing cancer through meditation!) Anxiety, tension, and aggressiveness decrease while stamina and ability to work are increased, along with inner-directed self-control and a general improvement in health. Mental functioning becomes clear, alert, integrated, and creative. And as the meditator grows in self-knowledge, as he finds his intrapersonal life becoming more harmonious and fulfilled, his family and social relations also tend to improve. These benefits have been reported many times in the literature on meditation and are being investigated by scientists around the world because of the recognized potential of the meditative life style for improving the physical, psychological, and social health of humanity.

Drug abuse is one problem area in which meditation is being used with increasing success. Studies are now under way at colleges and universities, rehabilitation hospitals, research institutes, and prisons to determine the reasons for this success, and resolutions have been passed by the Illinois and Kentucky legislatures urging meditation as a therapeutic and rehabilitative method. Since there are no reports of people giving up meditation in favor of drugs—but numerous reports of just the opposite—it seems clear that meditation is more effective than drugs in satisfying deep cravings for a sense of well-being and peace. Meditation corrects the problem by getting to root causes, producing a "natural high." Moreover, meditation is legal, inexpensive, requires no special equipment, is easily portable, and can be obtained in limitless quantity. Finally, meditation is harmless—except possibly for borderline psychotics, for whom meditation could precipitate a breakdown unless closely guided by an experienced teacher. Other than that, the worst that can happen is failure to meditate properly, in which case the meditator may simply lose interest. (If he is practical-minded, however, he will seek further advice and instruction. Resistances to the meditative experience can be dealt with through counseling.)

What Is Meditation?

The dictionary defines meditation as a type of conscious mental process. But that definition, based on Western psychology, is inadequate. The act of "contemplation" or "pondering" is not synonymous with meditation as a spiritual discipline. The Western literary tradition called meditation literature lies somewhere between the two. For example, the meditational poems of the English minister John Donne are deeply introspective and spiritual, approaching the mystical insights reported by others who have walked far along the path of a disciplined form of meditation. If we read further in the dictionary definition of meditation, we find a better sense in which it may be understood: "a form of private devotion consisting of deep, continued reflection on some religious theme." This is closer to the true meaning but is still not completely adequate to explain meditation.

In physiological terms meditation induces a fourth major state of consciousness. Neither waking, sleeping, nor dreaming, the meditation state has been described as a "wakeful hypometabolic condition." Brain waves, heartbeat, blood pressure, breathing, galvanic skin resistance, and many other factors are altered in meditation. Bodily functions slow to the point achieved in deep sleep, and sometimes beyond, yet the meditator remains awake and emerges from meditation with a feeling of rest and loss of stress or tension. (Here it should be understood that similarity or control of physiological processes—the art of the fakir—does not automatically grant spiritual growth and psychological maturity—the way of the yogi. Claims to the contrary, as seen in some advertisements for biofeedback devices and mind development courses, are highly misleading. Physiological control of nonconscious functions is often a byproduct of meditation, but it certainly is not the goal of meditation.)

THE CORE EXPERIENCE OF MEDITATION

The common core of all meditation experiences is an altered state of consciousness that leads to a diminishing (and hopefully total abolition) of ego, the self-centered sense of "I." This core experience state has been called relaxed attention or passive volition. To attain this state, many forms and techniques of meditation have been developed. Some are passive—for example, when a yogi sits cross-legged in a lotus position with so little motion that even his breathing is hard to detect. Other forms of meditation involve graceful body movements, such as *t'ai chi ch'uan* or the whirling dances of sufi dervishes. Sometimes the eyes are open in meditation; sometimes they are closed. Sometimes other sense organs are emphasized, as when beginners in Zen pay attention to their nasal breathing. In other traditions, however, sensory withdrawal is dominant. Some meditative techniques are silent; some are vocal. Transcendental Meditation is an example of the former, whereas the Krishna Consciousness Society uses the "Hare Krishna" ("Hail, Lord Krishna") chant, together with music and dancing. Some meditations are private, and some—such as a Quaker meeting—are public. Although most forms of meditation are self-directed, some are guided by a group leader.

The Types of Meditation

The silent forms of meditation use three techniques: concentration, contemplation, and mental repetition of a sound. The sound may be a single syllable such as *om*, or it may be a word, phrase, or verse from a holy text. The Tibetan Buddhist *Om mani padme hum* is an example. So is the simple prayer in *The Way of a Pilgrim*: "Lord Jesus Christ, have mercy on me." Many Christians use the Lord's Prayer as a basis for meditation. Kirpal Singh, an Indian sage, teaches his followers to repeat silently five names of God which he gives to them in a ceremony. In a similar fashion Maharishi Mahesh Yogi and the teachers he trains initiate people into Transcendental Meditation with various Sanskrit sounds said to be appropriate for their mental characteristics; the meditator silently repeats this *mantra* (in Sanskrit literally "hymn," "incantation") during his meditations. Zen Buddhism has a variety of meditative techniques, some of which involve use of a *koan*, an apparently insoluble riddle that the meditator mentally examines. A widely known *koan* asks, "What is the sound of one hand clapping?" (The correct translation of the ancient Japanese is

"the sound of a single hand.") Another inquires about
the basic nature of self-identity: "Who am I?"

In contemplative forms of meditation the eyes are
open so that the meditator sees a *yantra*, a form on
which he centers his consciousness. The focus of attention may be a religious object such as a crucifix,
statue, or picture. An inscription, a candle flame, a
flower, may also serve the purpose, or the meditator
may use a *mandala*, typically a square-in-a-circle design
of many colors, symbolizing the unity of microcosm
and macrocosm.

Concentration is generally considered the most difficult form of meditation. An image is visualized steadily
in the mind—say, the thousand-petal lotus of the
Hindu and Buddhist traditions or the crescent moon
of Islam or Judaism's Star of David or the Christian
mystic rose. Alternatively, the mind may be held free
of all imagery and "mental chatter"—a clearing away of
all thought. Or the attention may be focused at some
part of the body. Many people use the mystical "third
eye" at a point midway between the eyebrows, which
is said to coincide with the pineal gland. Also common
is the so-called concentration on your navel. This descriptive phrase is actually a misnaming of the process
of directing attention to the abdominal area and simply
becoming one with your breathing—the rhythmical,
cyclical body process by which life is sustained and
united with the universe.

Some disciplines combine different aspects of several meditative techniques. In its advanced stages ka-
rate and other martial arts use meditation in their
training regimen. Gurdjieff taught his students to combine movements and meditation. John Lilly, the
neurophysiologist–mind explorer, advocates dyadic
meditation in which two people sit silently facing each

other several feet apart, with their forefingers touching at the tips and their eyes gazing into each other. Ira Progoff, of Dialogue House in New York City, guides people through therapeutic sessions using a technique he developed called process meditation. It is usually performed in a group, and he speaks in order to guide the meditators into exploration of whatever imagery appears in their minds.

In the more advanced stages of meditation mental and physical stillness is complete. The meditator is totally absorbed in a blissful state of awareness having no particular object. His consciousness is without any thoughts or other contents; he is simply conscious of consciousness. In yoga this emptiness of consciousness without loss of consciousness is *samadhi*. In Zen it is called *satori*. In the West it is best known as cosmic consciousness or enlightenment. And it is paradoxical that in the emptiness comes a fullness—unity with divinity, knowledge of man's true nature, and "the peace that passeth understanding."

It should be apparent by now that meditation cannot be defined in a sentence or two. Patanjali, author of the ancient Sanskrit text *Yoga Sutras*, which first systematized yoga, explained raja yoga as being an eightfold path consisting of *yama* (moral disciplines), *niyama* (religious disciplines), *asana* (postures), *pranayama* (breathing exercises), *pratayahara* (releasing the mind from control by the senses), *dharana* (concentration), *dhyana* (meditation), and *samadhi*. The terms for "concentration" and "meditation" were used in a special way by Patanjali, and later writers have often employed them in a different sense, referring sometimes to a type of meditation and sometimes to a psychological state of meditation. In short, the term "meditation" is many things to many people, varying in this or that aspect, depending upon culture, religious traditions, psychological orientation, the individual's purpose, and other factors. It is not the definition but the experience that really matters.

TIME AND ATTITUDE

How long should you meditate? To begin, no more than thirty to forty minutes a day. Initiates in Transcendental Meditation meditate twice a day for periods of about twenty minutes. Likewise, beginners in Ananda Marga, a technique similar to Transcendental Meditation, follow almost the same schedule but are advised to participate in a group meditation once a week also. It is common in Zen to participate in a *sesshin*, a period of prolonged meditation lasting from a few days to several weeks. The meditators practice *zazen*—sitting meditation—in periods of twenty-five to forty minutes for ten to twelve hours a day. There are short periods of *kinhin*—walking meditation—in between. During *sesshin* everyone eats lightly, sleeps little, and avoids spoken or visual contact with everyone but the *roshi*, the master teacher. In India it is not rare for renunciates to spend eighteen hours or more daily in meditation—for years! Some even meditate around the clock, coming out of their meditation only for a short time to eat a minimal meal and then returning to their meditation in an immobile position which they maintain during sleep.

What is the right attitude for meditation? Spiritual masters agree: The best approach to meditation is one in which the meditator is essentially free from any desired end. It is similar to the process of learning for the sake of learning rather than for a reward. Goal-free learning for its own sake paradoxically produces the most skilled and creative people. Meditation should be performed in the same frame of mind—to help yourself grow as a human being, not simply to cure headaches or develop psychic powers. Many benefits will undoubtedly accrue in the process, but you should not lose sight of the fact that meditation is primarily a means to an end: enlightenment. It is a tool for learning spiritual psychology, a technique for expanding consciousness.

Here it is important to note that meditation does not require sacrifice or abandonment of the intellect. It is true that in meditation the intellect's limitations become apparent, and other (usually unsuspected) modes of creative problem-solving and insight emerge. However, enlightened teachers have always been recognized as brilliant people with finely honed intellectual powers who have enhanced their meditation "research" through scholarly studies. Their writings and discourses display clear logic, a keen analytic discrimination, and a knowledge of tradition. It is no accident, then, that students frequently report improvement in their grades and in their ability to study after beginning meditation.

Although enlightenment is the ultimate goal and is the result of a disciplined routine for a fairly extensive period—usually never less than several years—many meditators (perhaps most) will not reach this fulfillment. Nevertheless, if you are reasonably diligent and serious in your quest but for varying reasons you do not achieve a regularity and a frequency of the meditative experience, you will still find many worthwhile benefits in your life. These are likely to include (1) freedom from the feeling of pressure in day-to-day affairs, (2) avoidance of the "tired feeling," (3) minimal recurrence of chronic nagging pains such as headache, arthritis, sinusitis, indigestion, colitis, (4) reduction of insomnia, coffee dependence, tobacco dependence, and general use of drugs, (5) greater tolerance and love for others, (6) greater satisfaction from your religious affiliations (meditation is nondenominational—perhaps the one practice common to all major religions), and (7) a greater desire to be helpful, either in public service or in your own private life.

<h2>OBSTACLES TO MEDITATION</h2>

Some people are so obsessed with attaining heightened awareness that they make meditation almost the sole activity in their lives. This is not wise and is quite different from being steadfast in your meditation. Compulsive meditation is unlikely to lead to the highest spiritual levels. Enlightenment cannot be forced. It almost certainly will not happen if your attitude is "I *must* get enlightened!" as if enlightenment were some possession to be attained. Such mistaken thinking and misdirected desire is probably the greatest obstacle to successful meditation.

Another possible obstacle to enlightenment is the emergence of psychic powers. Meditators have frequently found that there comes a point in their development when psi ability is released. Extrasensory perception (ESP), psychokinesis (PK), and mediumistic powers manifest themselves. In the yogic tradition these are called *siddhis*. A guru strongly directs his trainees away from pursuit of any *siddhis* because they are a departure from the path toward the goal of yoga, divine union. The reason the guru does this is simple: Without enlightenment the psychic person is not ethically grounded and may not use his powers wisely. The result can be pain and suffering for himself and others. On the other hand, the enlightened have often found themselves in full control of a host of psychic powers without even trying, because it is a characteristic of higher consciousness, along with genius, artistic creativity, and literary talents.

Other obstacles to meditation may reside outside the meditative process. Since the goal of meditation is a transformation of the whole person, it is reasonable to assume that changes in various aspects of your life will affect the quality of your meditations. It is for this reason that teachers of meditation emphasize "right living" in a meditative life style: a healthy diet, an honest means of income, truthful speech, kindness and humility in relations with others, a social conscience, giving up egotistical desire for power, fame, prestige, and wealth, and so forth. Unless your total life is oriented to support the goal of your meditations, you are probably doing little more than wasting your time.

That does not mean, however, that successful meditation requires extreme asceticism and withdrawal from society. The true aim of meditation is to bring the meditator more fully into the world—not to retreat from it. A religious retreat may be appropriate for some in the course of their meditative training and discipline. This is the way of the anchorite, monk, and religious devotee—an honorable tradition. But the highest development in meditation—regardless of the "school" or "path"—brings technique and daily life together. When learning and living are integrated in spontaneous practice, the meditator is exhibiting what the Tibetan Buddhist teacher Chogyam Trungpa calls meditation in action. Meditation is no longer a tool or device, no longer just a "visit" to the fourth major state of consciousness. All four states are integrated in a manner of living that is best described as the fifth major state of consciousness. The meditator has so completely mastered the lessons of meditation that his entire life is a demonstration of the higher consciousness that can be experienced by each of us if sincerely sought.

MEDITATION AS (R)EVOLUTION

Such people have always been recognized as special individuals for whom attention and reverence are proper. In them meditation has led to a transformation of consciousness that is complete or nearly so. The act of changing consciousness also changes thought; changing thought changes behavior; and changing behavior changes society. Thus the changed ones live as examples to others who are on the way to transformation of self and world.

This is the fullest development of meditation. Personal evolution becomes social revolution. By changing yourself, you help to change the world.

Now listen to what some meditators from various traditions of both East and West have to tell us about starting on the path. . . .

What Is Meditation?

Hasten Slowly

Swami Chinmayananda

SWAMI CHINMAYANANDA *is an Indian teacher of Vedanta, the ancient system of Hindu philosophy. He has written many scholarly works on the* Bhagavad Gita, the Upanishads, *and* Vedanta. *He is represented in America by the Chinmaya Study Group in Napa, California.*

THE CRUELEST PERIODS for a sincere seeker during his spiritual life are the moments before the final experience-Divine. The pathetic anguish felt by him on the path is called "the dark night of the soul." This stage of extreme helplessness, complete disappointment, total dejection, and utter despair—though unavoidable—can be minimized if the seeker, on his meditation-flight to the transcendental, is well equipped and fully trained for this supreme, subjective adventure-Divine. It is the unprepared student who falls into unproductive, progress-halting ruts of thoughts and gets torn in the rising storms within him.

From *Meditation* (*Hasten Slowly*), by Swami Chinmayananda. Printed privately in 1972 and reprinted by permission of the author.

Throughout our Hindu spiritual literature there are scattered "pointers and sign posts" in order to guide the seekers who thus got stranded on the great path. Silhouetted against the dim light of our enthusiasm, each one of them presents but a vague shape of the pointing "hand" of the post. Everyone must pursue the pilgrimage in the direction so confidently shown by the unerring words of the Upanishads: all commentaries and explanations, annotations and discourses are attempts to raise a fluttering candle to the ambiguous crossroad signs left in the scriptures. . . .

Without all the preliminary preparations no one should start for a great pilgrimage. If one does so, it is clear that one has no sincerity, or sense of urgency, to reach the destination. The vehicle must be properly rigged, the fuel filled, the engine well tuned up, and the tools packed ready before one gets behind the wheel and drives away. The traveler must have the necessary technical knowledge to spot out troubles and correct them en route.

As we travel ahead we must be alert to read the road signs and obey implicitly their directions; nay, at places where one is in doubt, it will always be rewarding to slow down, even stop and get out, meet others on the road, inquire and ascertain whether one is traveling in the right direction. For a true and sincere seeker all these are useful hints, and a successful meditator of today among us is one who faithfully kept to this general plan of action.

The final peak of success aimed at by a mind in meditation is its own merger into the great "silence"— into the dynamic Pure Consciousness which is the "matrix" behind all the subtle world of subjective thoughts-and-emotions, and the gross realm of objective things-and-beings. The "conscious-thoughts," in their enlivened vitality, give us the apparent illusion of an individuality, known popularly as the ego (*jiva*).

Mind is the thought-flow in us. The quality, quantity, and direction of the thoughts in an individual determine the type of "flow" in him, and consequently it alone decides the worth, the beauty, and the effectiveness of his personality as expressed in life. All the psychiatric treatments doled out today are attempts to jerk the thought-flow of the patient into a rhythm. But the valleys cut by the long periods of wrong flow have created disturbing patterns of thought-gush in the subject, and he has an irresistible tendency to dash back into the old familiar stream of thinking and living. A spiritual seeker, to begin with, must therefore learn to initiate new and healthier channels of thought in himself and thereby, on the whole, etching vividly the desired scheme of a spiritually conducive mental behavior.

The direction of thoughts in a mind is determined by the peculiar subsurface motivating factors found within the emotional profile of each of us. These are called *vasanas*. When we are conscious of their pull, and when we realize that they are—at least some of them—conditioning us and dragging us into incompetency and into futile mental and physical dissipations, we call them "mental hangups." All of us have many such "hookups," and we struggle in vain against them, and ultimately, in our weariness, we come to yield to them. A spiritual seeker must conquer these *vasanas* in order to master his mind. Without this mastery over the thought-flow, self-expansion and self-experience are mere hopes, false dreams, empty claims, unprofitable bluffs.

The inner and subtler forces are more powerful than the outer and grosser factors ordering our lives and our world, and therefore, the *rishis* advise us first to learn to conquer, control, and tame the "outer equipments of perception"—the sense organs. And they are, in us, miserable slaves in their own chosen harem of enchanting objects. Remember, it is certainly excusable if the physical sense organs seek to fulfill themselves in the physical objects; for there is always a natural affinity for matter toward matter. But the individual personality should not get involved in them. So long as we live identified with the sense organs, and so completely committed to their passions, we can never wean ourselves away from the confusing medley of our riotous sense appetites for the sense objects.

In fact, the sense organs cannot function without the mind; and so, by raising the vision of the mind and engaging the mind entertainingly absorbed at a nobler altar of adoration, the sense organs can be clutched off, and their dash into the fields of sense objects can be slowed down. Yet the remedy suggested here is, in fact, not available to the raw seeker, because the mind as such cannot be readily lifted to a greater vision unless the motive forces functioning in it are purified and controlled.

The force that drives the mind to whip and herd the sense organs into the cesspool of sense objects is the intellect, and its various "schemes for happiness" called desires (*raga*). Again, these desires gurgling up in the intellect, poisoning the entire personality, are themselves manifestations of the ultimate source of all conditionings, the motivating urges deep in the "unconscious" in man, called the *vasanas*. This level of our personality is called by the *rishis* the "causal body" because it is the final determining factor that orders the type of mind and intellect, the "subtle body," and all behavior on the physical level, the "gross body."

The "causal" level of our personality—the unconscious depth-layer of our mind—is indicated in the Upanishadic discussions as nescience or ignorance (*avidya*). The "ignorance" of the spiritual essence, and its infinite glory and perfection, in us is the "cause" for our sense of restlessness, loneliness, fear, etc., and therefore the intellect "desires" for, the mind "agitates" with, and the sense organs "indulge" in the world of sense objects. The sense gratifications bring but more and more fatigue at all levels in the sensuous man, and never a deep, consoling satisfaction. Dissatisfied, the individual's intellect plans yet another desire, and the body sweats and toils again to seek and fulfill it—only to discover the same disconcerting sense of emptiness filling his heart, a painful weight of dissatisfaction crushing him in the end!

Sooner or later one realizes, if intelligent, that all the wealth acquired, all objects of pleasures procured, all relationships maintained, name and fame gained, work done, achievements accomplished—none of them has any relevance to the inner actual peace and joy lived. The entire life then seems an empty struggle, a futile exertion, a meaningless mission.

Thus, the *rishis* pithily declare that the pangs of life lived by the many are all due to their own spiritual "ignorance" (*avidya*), consisting of the irresistibly compelling urges to love, to acquire, and to enjoy the world around. The removal of this "ignorance" (*avidya*) is the goal of meditation. With the knowledge (*vidya*) of the spiritual center, the Self, this "ignorance" is ended. "Seek the Self" is the silent scream of the highest meditation.

On this grand path of spirituality, hasten slowly.

The Aim of Meditation

Gopi Krishna

GOPI KRISHNA *is an Indian yogi-scientist-philosopher.*
He lives in Srinagar, Kashmir, and is represented in
America by the Kundalini Research Foundation in
New York City. His books include Kundalini, The
Biological Basis of Religion and Genius, *and* The Secret
of Yoga.

WHAT I AM PRESENTING BEFORE YOU now is based on a
remarkable experience I had thirty-five years ago, which
has continued undiminished till now. This experience
shows that there is a divine key, a psychosomatic lever
in the human brain and nervous system, which, with
meditation, worship, and prayer—coupled with self-
discipline—can lead to a beatific state of higher consciousness.

It is safe to assume that the desire for meditation is
an innate tendency of the human mind and has been
in evidence for thousands of years. Meditation, in the

This unpublished article is based on a talk delivered over
German television in 1971 and is printed by permission of the
Kundalini Research Foundation, 10 East Thirty-ninth Street,
New York, N.Y. 10016.

generally accepted sense of the term, is concentration with a spiritual objective.

Patanjali, the most renowned authority on yoga in India, divides meditation into three parts: *dharana*, which means concentration in the preliminary stage; *dhyana*, which means stabilized concentration for a certain length of time; and *samadhi*, which means complete absorption in one thought or object to the exclusion of every other thought and even sense impression.

During *samadhi* one becomes oblivious to the world. The object of developing the practice of meditation to the point where only one object remains as the focus of attention, and all other flow is arrested, is to create a condition of stillness in the mind so that the reality behind our thoughts, fancies, passions, and desires becomes manifest. When this unveiling occurs, a new, glorious world opens before the inner vision of the seeker.

A definite tendency to absorbed states of mind is also noticed in children and infants at times. We often see them looking at some object that has excited their curiosity, with an expression of deep absorption, as if trying to probe into the very depth of it. Sometimes the state of absorption is so deep that the least disturbing noise or the close approach of somebody wakes them up from their abstraction with a start.

The idea prevalent in many countries is that the child has the possibility of entering into other planes of being, enwrapping it in golden dreams and visions which it sees and raptly contemplates at times. This can be possible because the mind of a child is not too much agitated by the fret and fever of the world. The human child, during its growth, not only repeats the aeonian history of the race but also symbolizes the distant future of mankind by its occasional beautiful, abstracted states, pointing to the age when man shall have learned to explore the inner universe of consciousness. This inner world is far more extended and more marvelous than the universe perceived with our senses.

In all intellectual and creative work concentration and absorption play a most important role. In fact, creative talent or genius is inseparable from absorption. We have heard or read stories about the intense states of absorption of men of genius, like Newton and Einstein. During the creative periods of a talented man, an abrupt interruption or disturbance not only is highly disagreeable but may also cause a shock.

I mention these facts to show that meditation or sustained concentration is a natural process. The same is true when meditation is used for God-realization. If we now turn to average men and women, we find here also that it is the moments of intense absorption that provide them with the happiest, most beautiful, and most harmonious intervals in their lives. A few illustrations are enough to make this clear. Everyone knows with what concentrated attention one reads a most interesting and fascinating novel or story. We are absorbed in it heart and soul for the time being and, not infrequently, postpone our other work just to have the time to complete it without disturbance and distraction.

When we listen enraptured to music, when we see a masterpiece of painting or sculpture, when we watch a fascinating drama or a motion picture, when we see a grand panorama of nature, when we read of the exploits of space travelers and, from their eyes, see the pictures of our earth as a small rotating globe far away, we often enter into deep, absorbed states of our mind. It is then that we forget ourselves and our surroundings in the intensity of our feelings. The same happens in the play of love. We forget ourselves and the world in the ecstasy of this contact and remain in a state of intense absorption during all the period while the contact lasts, forgetting even the flow of time.

I have dwelt on these aspects of deep engrossment of our attention to show that apart from its religious or spiritual significance, meditation or a deep state of absorption of the mind plays a signal role in our lives. But why is this state of deep concentration necessary for the intellectual and the genius for their creative activity and also for average men and women for the happiest, most thrilling, and most beautiful moments in their lives? It is because of such moments that we come nearer to our soul, the fountainhead of all knowledge, all science, all art, all music, all happiness, and all the exquisite sensations that we enjoy. They do not come from our learning, skill, or practice or from the instruments and objects that we employ, but from the unfathomed depths of our own being, which is a drop in the ocean of infinite existence.

All spiritual exercises and all methods of meditation, all modes of worship and prayer, enjoined by the founders of religions and great spiritual teachers, are directed to achieve one purpose, and that is to reach the deeper levels of the soul and through it to the Universal Spirit, the Eternal Source of all. The mystic in trance or the yogi in *samadhi* attains to a state of concentration where he is entirely absorbed in the contemplation of this source of all beauty, all harmony, all life, and all happiness in the universe. It is for this reason that it is called *sat-chit-ananda*, or existence-consciousness-bliss, by the Indian sages. It is a concentrated state of blissful consciousness, impossible to describe.

It might be asked what are the surest means and infallible methods to reach this glorious cosmic plane of being in which the individual lives constantly in contact with his immortal soul, free from fear and grief. I have no answer to this question, nor, to the best of my knowledge, is there a positive answer in the revealed scriptures of any faith—not in the Bible, the Vedas, the Gita, the Koran, nor in any other scripture.

The reason is that we do not deal here with material objectives. We do not aspire here to have wealth, to cross an ocean, to make a discovery, to climb a mountain, to gain power, or to visit the moon. Here we are aspiring to gain approach to the ocean of consciousness that feeds all life in the universe, the Creator, and it is not we who can decide when the audience will be granted. All we can do is to hope, to aspire, to make the right effort, to have the longing in our heart, and to shape our whole life in a way to make this dream possible.

There is no secret entrance, no royal road, no magic key, to reach the author of our being. We have to try for it with all our heart and soul and leave the decision in His hands. There is no magical formula or mantra or secret method of meditation that can work miracles and carry us to higher states of consciousness by the momentum of our own efforts without divine grace. This is a point on which all religions and religious disciplines are agreed. The door must be opened from the inside. We cannot force it.

A realization of this point is of greatest importance in our approach to meditation and choice of the methods employed and practiced. We should realize that we can only knock at the door and continue knocking until our prayer is heard and the door is unlocked. An understanding of this fact can be of greatest help to us and save us from pain and disappointment.

Viewed from this angle, meditation becomes a vital part of our lives, a lifelong occupation, a permanent duty that we owe. We have not to hurry, we have not to find magical methods, but we have to tune our mind so that the thought of the Divine is never far from it. We can attend to all our occupations and duties without the least hindrance and, perhaps, even more efficiently if divine thoughts always occupy a place at the back of our minds. This is sahaja yoga, the easiest and most effective form of spiritual discipline. Sahaja yoga is prescribed by every great religious teacher of the past. This is what Christ means when he says to love your God with all your heart and soul, because a beloved object occupies a permanent place in the thoughts of the lover. When we are able to think of a beloved sweetheart a hundred times a day, without impairing the efficiency of our work, we should also be able to do it with the Divine if our thirst is real.

This is the safest method, for no force is necessary. The mind can become habituated to it with slow, gradual practice. As I have said, this has to be a lifelong practice and search. The constant remembrance of God, the holiest of the holy, is to be followed by purity in thought and conduct. The world has not to be given up, the desires have not to be totally denied. They are also a part of human life.

But moderation has to be exercised to keep the thought of God. Otherwise desires and passions consume all our energy and time. Moderation and purity of mind are therefore essential and form an integral part of meditation.

But what is the basis for this desire for meditation, this urge to attain an inner state of peace and beatitude or to experience God? This is because our brains are still evolving, because mankind has to reach a higher state of consciousness for which there is a special arrangement in the brain and the nervous system of man. This mechanism is not yet known to scholars. It is my earnest wish to make this divine power-reservoir known to the world of science.[1]

It is because of this possibility in our brain that our meditational exercises succeed. It is necessary that this knowledge become well known because once it is known, meditation for gaining a higher state of consciousness by stimulating this center in the brain will become an integral part of human life, leading to a glorious state of consciousness, conducive to peace and happiness of the world.

[1] This topic is discussed in detail in the author's autobiography, *Kundalini* (Berkeley: Shambhala, 1971), *The Biological Basis of Religion and Genius* (New York: Harper & Row, 1972), and *The Secret of Yoga* (New York: Harper & Row, 1972). *Editor.*

The Domain of Meditation

Claudio Naranjo

CLAUDIO NARANJO *is a research psychiatrist associated with the University of California's Institute of Personality Assessment and Research. He has published one other book,* The One Quest, *which examines ancient and modern systems of meditation.*

THE WORD "MEDITATION" has been used to designate a variety of practices that differ enough from one another so that we may find trouble in defining what *meditation* is.

Is there a commonality among the diverse disciplines alluded to by this same word? Something that makes them only different forms of a common endeavor? Or are these various practices only superficially related by their being individual spiritual exercises? The latter, apparently, is the point of view of those who have chosen to equate meditation with only a certain type of practice, ignoring all the others that do not fit their description or definition. It is thus that in the Christian tradition meditation is most often understood as a dwelling upon certain *ideas*, or engaging in a directed intellectual course of activity; while some of those who are more familiar with Eastern methods of meditation equate the matter with a dwelling on anything *but* ideas, and with the attainment of an aconceptual state of mind that excludes intellectual activity. Richard of St. Victor, the influential theorist of meditation of the Christian Middle Ages, drew a distinction between meditation and contemplation according to purposefulness and the part played by reason:

> Meditation with great mental industry plods along the steep and laborious road keeping the end in view. Contemplation on a free wing circles around with great nimbleness wherever the impulse takes it. . . . Meditation investigates, contemplation wonders.[1]

Other authors distinguish concentration from meditation, regarding the former as a mere drill for the latter. An interesting case of restriction of the term appears in Kapleau's *The Three Pillars of Zen*.[2] He insists that *zazen* is not to be confused with meditation. This is a paradoxical proposition, since the very word *zen*, from the Chinese *ch'an*, ultimately derives from the concept of *dhyana*, meditation. Zen Buddhism is, therefore, meditation Buddhism in a real and practical sense. Yet the distinction is understandable in view of the apparent diversity of forms that meditation has taken, even within Buddhism.

[1] Richard of St. Victor, *De Gratia Contemplationis sen Benjamin Major*, I, 3, in *Selected Writings on Contemplation*, trans. Claire Kirchberger (London: 1957).

[2] Philip Kapleau, ed., *The Three Pillars of Zen* (Boston: Beacon, 1965).

The distinction between ideational versus non-ideational is only one of the many contrasting interpretations of the practices called meditation. Thus, while certain techniques (like those in the Tibetan tantra) emphasize mental images, others discourage paying attention to any imagery; some involve sense organs and use visual forms (*mandalas*) or music, and others emphasize a complete withdrawal from the senses; some call for complete inaction, and others involve action (*mantra*), gestures (*mudra*), walking, or other activities. Again, some forms of meditation require the summoning up of specific feeling states, while others encourage an indifference beyond the identification with any particular illusion.

The very diversity of practices given the name of "meditation" by the followers of this or that particular approach is an invitation to search for the answer of what meditation is *beyond its forms*. And if we are not content just to trace the boundaries of a particular group of related techniques, but instead search for a unity within the diversity, we may indeed recognize such a unity in an *attitude*. We may find that, *regardless of the medium* in which meditation is carried out—whether images, physical experiences, verbal utterances, etc.—the task of the meditator is essentially the same, as if the many forms of practice were nothing more than different occasions for the same basic exercise.

If we take this step beyond a behavioral definition of meditation in terms of a *procedure*, external or even internal, we may be able to see that meditation cannot be equated with thinking or non-thinking, with sitting still or dancing, with withdrawing from the senses or waking up the senses: meditation is concerned with the development of a *presence*, a modality of being, which may be expressed or developed in whatever situation the individual may be involved.

This presence or mode of being transforms whatever it touches. If its medium is movement, it will turn into dance; if stillness, into living sculpture; if thinking, into the higher reaches of intuition; if sensing, into a merging with the miracle of being; if feeling, into love; if singing, into sacred utterance; if speaking, into prayer or poetry; if doing the things of ordinary life, into a ritual in the name of God or a celebration of existence. Just as the spirit of our times is technique-oriented in its dealings with the external world, it is technique-oriented in its approach to psychological or spiritual reality. Yet, while numerous schools propound this or that method as a solution of human problems, we know that it is not merely the method but *the way in which it is employed* that determines its effectiveness, whether in psychotherapy, art, or education. The application of techniques or tools in an interpersonal situation depends upon an almost intangible "human factor" in the teacher, guide, or psychotherapist. When the case is that of the intrapersonal method of meditation, the human factor beyond the method becomes even more elusive. Still, as with other techniques, it is the *how* that counts more than the *what*. The question of the right attitude on the part of the meditator is the hardest for meditation teachers to transmit, and though it is the object of most supervision, may be apprehended only through practice.

It might be said that the attitude, or "inner posture," of the meditator is both his path and his goal. For the subtle, invisible *how* is not merely a *how to meditate* but a *how to be*, which in meditation is exercised in a simplified situation. And precisely because of its elusive quality beyond the domain of an instrumentality that may be described, the attitude that is the heart of meditation is generally sought after in the most simple external or "technical" situations: in stillness, silence, monotony, "just sitting." Just as we do not see the stars in daylight, but only in the absence of the sun, we may never taste the subtle essence of meditation in the daylight of ordinary activity in all its complexity. That essence may be revealed when we have suspended everything else but *us*, our presence, our attitude, beyond any activity or the lack of it. Whatever the outer situation, the inner task is simplified, so that nothing remains to do but gaze at a candle, listen to the hum in our own ears, or "do nothing." We may then discover that there are innumerable ways of gazing, listening, doing nothing; or, conversely, innumerable ways of *not* just gazing, not just listening, not just sitting. Against the background of the simplicity required by the exercise, we may become aware of ourselves and all that we bring to the situation, and we may begin to grasp experientially the question of attitude.

While practice in most activities implies the development of habits and the establishment of conditioning, the practice of meditation can be better understood as quite the opposite: a persistent effort to detect and become free from all conditioning, compulsive functioning of mind and body, habitual emotional responses that may contaminate the utterly simple situation required by the participant. This is why it may be said that the attitude of the meditator is both his path and his goal: the unconditioned state is the freedom of attainment and also the target of every single effort. What the meditator realizes in his practice is to a large extent how he is failing to meditate properly, and by becoming aware of his failings he gains understanding and the ability to let go of his wrong way. The right

way, the desired attitude, is what remains when we
have, so to say, stepped out of the way.

If meditation is above all the pursuit of a certain
state of mind, the practice of a certain attitude toward
experience that transcends the qualities of this or that
particular experience, a mental process rather than a
mental content, let us then attempt to say what cannot be said, and speak of what this common core of
meditation is.

A trait that all types of meditation have in common,
even at the procedural level, gives us a clue to the attitude we are trying to describe: all meditation is a
dwelling upon something.

While in most of one's daily life the mind flits from
one subject or thought to another, and the body moves
from one posture to another, meditation practices
generally involve an effort to stop this merry-go-round
of mental or other activity and to set our attention
upon a single object, sensation, utterance, issue, mental
state, or activity.

"Yoga," says Patanjali in his second aphorism, "is the
inhibition of the modifications of the mind." As you
may gather from this statement, the importance of
dwelling upon something is not so much in the *something* but in the *dwelling upon*. It is this concentrated
attitude that is being cultivated, and, with it, attention
itself. Though all meditation leads to a stilling of the
mind as described by Patanjali, it does not always consist in a voluntary attempt to stop all thinking or other
mental activity. As an alternative, the very interrup-
tions to meditation may be taken as a temporary
meditation object, by dwelling upon them. There is,
for example, a Theravadan practice that consists in
watching the rising and falling of the abdomen during
the breathing cycle. While acknowledging these move-

ments, the meditator also acknowledges anything else that may enter his field of consciousness, whether sensations, emotions, or thoughts. He does it by mentally naming three times that of which he has become aware ("noise, noise, noise," "itching, itching, itching") and returning to the rising and falling. As one meditation instructor put it: "There is no disturbance because any disturbance can be taken as a meditation object. Anger, worry, anxiety, fear, etc., when appearing should not be suppressed but should be accepted and acknowledged with awareness and comprehension. This meditation is for dwelling in clarity of consciousness and full awareness."

The practice described above is a compromise of freedom and constraint in the direction of attention, in that the meditator periodically returns to the "fixation point" of visual awareness of his respiratory movements. If we should take one further step toward freedom from a pre-established structure, we would have a form of meditation in which the task would be merely to be aware of the contents of consciousness at the moment. Though this openness to the present might appear to be the opposite of the concentrated type of attention required by gazing at a candle flame, it is not so. Even the flame as an object of concentration is an ever-changing object that requires, because of its very changeability, that the meditator be in touch with it moment after moment, in sustained openness to the present. But closer still is a comparison between the observation of the stream of consciousness and concentration on music. In the latter instance, we can clearly recognize that a focusing of attention is not only compatible with, but indispensable to, a full grasp of the inflections of sound.

Our normal state of mind is one that might be

compared to an inattentive exposure to music. The mind is active, but only intermittently are we aware of the present. A real awakening to the unfolding of our psychic activity requires an effort of attention greater and not lesser than that demanded by attending to a fixed "object" like an image, verbal repetition, or a region of the body. In fact, it is because attention to the spontaneous flow of psychological events is so difficult that concentrative meditation *sensu stricto* is necessary either as an alternative or as a preliminary.

Attending to one's breath, for instance, by counting and remaining undistracted by the sensations caused by the air in one's nose, is a much more "tangible" object of consciousness than feeling-states and thoughts, and by persisting we may discover the difference between true awareness and the fragmentary awareness that we ordinarily take to be complete. After acquiring a taste of "concentrated state" in this situation and some insight into the difficulties that it entails, we may be more prepared for the observation of "inner states."

Such a "taste" can be regarded as a foretaste or, rather, a diluted form of the taste the knowledge of which might be the end result of meditation. In the terminology of yoga, that ultimate state is called *samadhi,* and it is regarded as the natural development of *dhyana,* the meditative state, itself the result of an enhancement or development of *dharana,* concentration. *Dharana,* in turn, is regarded as a step following *pranayama,* the technique of breathing control particular to yoga, which entails just such a concentrative effort as the spontaneous breathing of Buddhist meditation.

The process leading from simple concentration to the goal of meditation (*samadhi, kensho,* or whatever we may want to call it) is thus one of progressive refinement. By practicing attention we understand better and better what attention is; by concentrating or condensing the taste of meditation known to us we come closer and closer to its essence. Through this process of enhancing that *attitude* which is the gist of the practice, we enter states of mind that we may regard as unusual and, at the same time, as the very ground or core of what we consider our ordinary experience. We would have no such "ordinary" experience without awareness, for instance, but the intensification of awareness leads us to a perspective as unfamiliar as that of the world which intensified scientific knowledge reveals to us—a world without any of the properties evident to our senses, materiality itself included.

Awareness, though, is only a facet of that meditative state into whose nature we are inquiring. Or, at least, it is only a facet if we understand the term as we usually do. The meditator who sets out to sharpen his awareness of awareness soon realizes that awareness is inseparable from other aspects of experience for which we have altogether different words, and so intertwined with them that it could be regarded as only conceptually independent from them.

Let us take the classical triad *sat-chit-ananda* according to the formulations of Vedanta, for instance. On the basis of the experiential realizations in which we are interested here, these three are our true nature and that of everything else, and the three are inseparable aspects of a unity: *sat* means being; *chit*, consciousness of mind; *ananda*, bliss.

From our ordinary point of view, these three seem quite distinct: we can conceive of being without bliss or awareness, of awareness without bliss. From the point of view of what to us is an unusual or "altered" state of consciousness, on the other hand, the individual sees his very identity in another light, so that he *is* consciousness. His very being is his act of awareness, and this act of awareness is not bliss-ful but consists *in* bliss. While we ordinarily speak of pleasure as a reaction in *us* to *things*, the meditator in *samadhi* experiences no distinction between himself, the world, and the quality of his experience because he *is* his experience, and experience is of the nature of bliss. From his point of view, the ordinary state of consciousness is one of not truly experiencing, of not being in contact with the world or self, and, to that extent, not only deprived of bliss but comparable to a non-being.

Special states of consciousness are not more expressible than states of consciousness in general, and are bound to the same limitation that we can only understand what we have already experienced. Since the goal of meditation is precisely something beyond the bounds of our customary experience, anything that we might understand would probably be something that it is not, and an attachment to the understanding could only prevent our progress. This is why many traditions have discouraged descriptions, avoided images or positive formulations of man's perfected state or of the deity, and stressed either practice or *negative* formulations:

> It is named Invisible, Infinite, and Unbounded, in such terms as may indicate not what It is, but what It is not: for this, in my judgment, is more in accord with its nature, since, as the capital mysteries and the priestly traditions suggested, we are right in saying that It is not in the likeness of any created thing, and we cannot comprehend Its super-essential, invisible, and ineffable infinity. If, therefore, the negations in the descriptions of

the divine are true, and the affirmations are inconsistent
with It. . . .

—Dionysius the Areopagite

The teacher [Gautama] has taught that a "becoming"
and a "non-becoming" are destroyed; therefore it ob-
tains that: *nirvana is neither an existent thing nor an
unexistent thing.*

—Nagarjuna

Never, never teach virtue . . . you will walk in
danger, beware! beware!

Every man knows how useful it is to be useful.

No one seems to know how useful it is to be useless.

—Chuang-tzu

Yet positive formulations of what existence looks or
feels like in peak states of consciousness abound. When
these are conceptual (as in terms of *sat-chit-ananda*
or other trinities), they constitute the experiential core
of theologies, theistic or non-theistic. When symbolic,
they constitute true religious art, and some great art
that we do not conventionally consider "religious."
Both types of expression are important to consider in
any attempt like ours, which is not properly one of
"expressing" but of determining the psychological characteristics of the meditational state. Moreover, the
symbols of the meditative state are part of the practice
of meditation itself in some of its forms, and we could
not bypass their significance in any account of such
disciplines.

Though, theoretically, any meditation object could
suffice and be equivalent to any other, particular objects of meditation serve (especially for one not far
advanced in the practice) the double function of a
target of attention and a reminder of that right attitude which is both the path and the goal of meditation.

Just as our experience shows that certain poems, musical works, or paintings can hold our interest without being exhausted while others soon enter the category of the obvious, typical meditation objects partake of the quality of becoming more rather than less after repeated contemplations. A Buddhist *sutra* or a Christian litany, the symbol of the cross or the Star of David, the rose or the lotus, have not persisted as objects of meditation on the basis of tradition alone but on the grounds of a special virtue, a built-in appropriateness and richness, which meditators have discovered again and again throughout the centuries. Being symbols created by a higher state of consciousness, they evoke their source and always lead the meditator beyond his ordinary state of mind, a beyondness that is the meditator's deepest self, and the presence of which is the very heart of meditation.

We must not forget, however, that symbols, meditation objects, or "seeds" (*bija*) for meditation are only a technique. In contrast to the *directive* approach to meditation, in which the individual places himself under the influence of a symbol, we find a *non-directive* approach in which the person lets himself be guided by the promptings of his own deeper nature. Instead of letting a symbol shape his experience, he attends to his experience as given to his awareness, and by persisting in the attempt he finds that his perceptions undergo a progressive refinement. Instead of holding on to a rigid form handed down by tradition, he dwells upon the form that springs from his own spontaneity, until he may eventually find that in his own soul lies hidden the source of all traditions.

Still another alternative to the guiding influence of the symbol may be found in a purely negative approach, which is directive too, but only in a restrictive sense: instead of taking an object to dwell upon and identify with, the meditator here puts his effort in *moving away* from all objects, in *not* identifying with anything that he perceives. By departing from the known he thus allows for the unknown, by excluding the irrelevant he opens himself up to the relevant, and by dis-identifying from his current self concept, he may go into the aconceptual awakening of his true nature.

The three types of meditation may be represented as the three points of a triangle (as in Figure 1). At

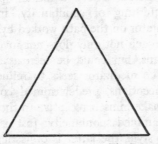

The Negative Way: elimination, detachment, emptiness, centered, the "middle way"

The Way of Forms: concentration, absorption, union, outer-directed, Apollonian

The Expressive Way: freedom, transparence, surrender, inner-directed, Dionysian

Figure 1

one end of the base (line) is represented meditation upon externally given symbolic objects, and at the other end is the contrasting alternative of meditation upon spontaneously arising contents of the mind. In the former, the person confronts an *other* (idea of

God, etc.) upon which he concentrates, in which he sees his own center, with which he identifies, and to which he seems receptive. In the latter, the meditator seeks to become receptive to, and to identify with, *himself*, without the mirror device of the symbol.

In the former approach the individual attempts to interiorize an externally given form, or projects his experience onto it, until his subjectivity is absorbed by the object. In the latter, the individual seeks attunement to an inner form or a formless depth out of which a personal form emerges—in imagery, thoughts, gestures, feelings, or, above all, as an attitude toward the situation at the moment. The former is an assimilative, introjective, or projective process. The latter, a process of expression. One is a formal approach that involves relinquishing of spontaneity, insofar as it keeps the meditator on the path worked by the symbol. The other approach not only does not involve extrinsically given forms, but could be seen as a pursuit of formlessness: the meditator seeks to relinquish expectations, preconceptions, predetermined courses of action, so as to make himself receptive to the promptings of his unprogrammed spontaneity. Just as the former is of a hieratic style, the latter is orgiastic; the former entails obedience to a pattern, the latter, freedom from the known; the former is Apollonian, the latter Dionysian.

Different as these two may seem, they converge upon a common end state, for, after all, the forms and symbols that the traditions of mankind offer as starting points for meditation have originated in spontaneity. And, conversely, a surrender to spontaneity leads not to chaos but to the expression of a definite structure that all men share. As Jung showed in the domain of visual fantasy, the images become more "collective"—

and therefore similar to the universal patterns of myth —the more the subject explores his presumably individual depth.

In contrast with these two orientations in the task of meditation—one outer-directed and the other inner-directed—the third point in our triangle stands for a purely *negative* approach: not a reaching out or a reaching in, but a self-emptying. In this approach the effort is to attain a stillness of the mind's conceptualizing activity, a withdrawal from external perceptions and internal experience alike, to cultivate a detachment toward psychological acting in general. This method is based upon the experiential finding that the state we call wakefulness is in large measure of an inhibiting nature, so that our ordinary mental operations actively preclude or limit the occurrence of states such as those pursued in meditation. If we are able to accomplish nothing more than a stilling of the mind, bringing the goal-directed activity of our ordinary state of consciousness to a standstill, separating temporarily from our ego functions (and still retain consciousness), we may enter an altogether unfamiliar domain of experience without ever having sought it *positively* (i.e., approached it as a goal known through symbolical or conceptual formulations).

The Art of Meditation

Alan Watts

ALAN WATTS (1915–73) *helped introduce Zen to the Western world. He is the author of many books on religion and philosophy, including* Psychotherapy East and West, The Two Hands of God, *and an autobiography,* In My Own Way.

"The dewdrop slips into the shining sea."
SIR EDWIN ARNOLD, *The Light of Asia*

THE PRACTICE OF MEDITATION is not what is ordinarily meant by "practice," in the sense of repetitious preparation for some future performance. It may seem odd and illogical to say that meditation in the form of yoga, *dhyana,* or *zazen,* as used by Hindus and Buddhists, is a practice without purpose—in some future time—because it is the art of being completely centered in the here and now. "I'm not sleepy, and there is no place I'm going to."

We are living in a culture entirely hypnotized by the illusion of time, in which the so-called present moment is felt as nothing but an infinitesimal hairline between an all-powerfully causative past and an absorbingly important future. We have no present. Our consciousness is almost completely preoccupied with memory and expectation. We do not realize that there never was, is, or will be any other experience than present experience.

We are therefore out of touch with reality. We confuse the world as talked about, described, and measured with the world that actually is. We are sick with a fascination for the useful tools of names and numbers, of symbols, signs, conceptions, and ideas. Meditation is therefore the art of suspending verbal and symbolic thinking for a time, somewhat as a courteous audience will stop talking when a concert is about to begin.

Simply sit down, close your eyes, and listen to all sounds that may be going on—without trying to name or identify them. Listen as you would listen to music. If you find that verbal thinking will not drop away, don't attempt to stop it by force of willpower. Just keep your tongue relaxed, floating easily in the lower jaw, and listen to your thoughts as if they were birds chattering outside—mere noise in the skull—and they will eventually subside of themselves, as a turbulent and muddy pool will become calm and clear if left alone.

Also, become aware of breathing and allow your lungs to work in whatever rhythm seems congenial to them. And for a while just sit listening and feeling breath. But if possible, don't *call* it that. Simply experience the nonverbal happening. You may object that this is not "spiritual" meditation but mere attention to the "physical" world, but it should be understood that the spiritual and the physical are only ideas, philosophical conceptions, and that the reality of which you are now aware is not an idea. Furthermore, there is no "you" aware of it. That was also just an idea. Can you hear yourself listening?

And then begin to let your breath "fall" out, slowly and easily. Don't force or strain your lungs, but let the breath come out in the same way that you let yourself slump into a comfortable bed. Simply let it go, go, and go. As soon as there is the least strain, just let it come back in as a reflex; don't pull it in. Forget the clock. Forget to count. Just keep it up for as long as you feel the luxury of it.

Using the breath in this way, you discover how to generate energy without force. For example, one of the gimmicks (in Sanskrit, *upaya*) used to quiet the thinking mind and its compulsive chattering is known as *mantra*—the chanting of sounds for the sake of sound rather than meaning. Therefore, begin to "float" a single tone on the long, easy outbreak at whatever pitch is most comfortable. Hindus and Buddhists use for this practice such syllables as *om, ah, hum* (i.e., *hung*), and Christians might prefer *amen* or *alleluia*, Muslims *Allah*, and Jews *Adonai*: it really makes no difference, since what is important is simply and solely the sound. Like Zen Buddhists, you could use just the syllable *mooo* (*mu*). Dig *that*, and let your consciousness sink down, down, down, into the sound for as long as there is no sense of strain.

Above all, don't look for a result, for some marvelous change of consciousness or *satori*: the whole essence of meditation-practice is centering upon what is —not on what should or might be. The point is not to make the mind blank or to concentrate fiercely upon, say, a single point of light—although that, too, can be delightful without the fierceness.

For how long should this be kept up? My own, and perhaps unorthodox, feeling is that it can be continued for as long as there is no sensation of forcing it—and this may easily extend to thirty or forty minutes at one sitting, whereafter you will want to return to the state of normal restlessness and distraction.

In sitting for meditation, it is best to use a substantial cushion on the floor, to keep the spine erect but not stiff, to have the hands on the lap—palms upward—resting easily upon each other, and to sit cross-legged like a Buddha figure, either in full or in half lotus posture, or kneeling and sitting back on the heels. "Lotus" means placing one or both feet sole-upward upon the opposite thigh. These postures are slightly uncomfortable, but they have, therefore, the advantage of keeping you awake!

In the course of meditation you may possibly have astonishing visions, amazing ideas, and fascinating fantasies. You may also feel that you are becoming clairvoyant or that you are able to leave your body and travel at will. But all that is distraction. Leave it alone and simply watch what happens *now*. One does not meditate in order to acquire extraordinary powers, for if you managed to become omnipotent and omniscient, what would you do? There would be no further surprises for you, and your whole life would be like making love to a plastic partner. Beware, then, of all those gurus who promise "marvelous results" and other future benefits from their disciplines. The whole point is to realize that there *is* no future and that the real sense of life is an exploration of the eternal now. *Stop, look,* and *listen!* Or shall we say, "Turn on, tune in, and drop *in*"?

A story is told of a man who came to the Buddha with offerings of flowers in both hands. The Buddha said, "Drop it!" So he dropped the flowers in his left hand. The Buddha said again, "Drop it!" He dropped the flowers in his right hand. And the Buddha said, "Drop that which you have neither in the right nor in the left, but in the middle!" And the man was instantly enlightened.

It is marvelous to have the sense that all living and moving is dropping, or going along with gravity. After all, the earth is falling around the sun, and, in turn, the sun is falling around some other star. For energy is precisely a taking of the line of least resistance. Energy is mass. The power of water is in following its own weight. All comes to him who weights.

Entering the World of Meditation

Swami Nitya Chaitanya Yati

SWAMI NITYA CHAITANYA YATI *is head of the Nara-yana Gurukala Movement, an effort conceived as a contemplative worldwide fraternity to awaken people to the spiritual aspects of life. As a young man, Swami Nitya served Mahatma Gandhi. He holds a master's degree in philosophy and has been head of a psychology department in college, director of the Institute of Psychic and Spiritual Research in New Delhi, and head of the interdisciplinary research studies in yoga for the Indian Council on Medical Research. His ashram is located in Varkala, Kerala, India.*

WE HEAR OF MANY MEDITATION TECHNIQUES. Most of the techniques are specially made for America, but there is really no technique for meditation, and yet we can say that there are techniques. It all depends on what you seek. There is nothing called meditation for meditation's sake.

This word "meditation" is a very vague term. We

"Entering the World of Meditation" is transcribed from an extemporaneous talk given in April 1973 to a group of psychiatrists in Portland, Oregon, and is printed by permission.

do not even differentiate meditation from contemplation. If you are using your mind and going deeper and
deeper into the meaning, significance, or value of a
certain reasoning or perception or even a certain conceptual knowledge, then you are only contemplating;
you are not meditating.

We have to first see the mechanism of our own mind
and how it works. That's our instrument, and if we are
going to use that instrument to bring about a certain
result, we have first to visualize that result. This visualization of the value structure to which you want to
apply your mind is called a unitive philosophical vision.
Unitive in Sanskrit is called *yoga*. A philosophical vision is called *darsana*. So this is called *yoga darsana*.
One should have a unitive vision in which there is a
central value to which all other values are related in
a harmonious way. There are gradations, hierarchies,
and ensembles of values.

Once you know this is what you really want, then
you need a methodologically correct approach to it.
The correct approach is through the exploitation of a
possibility, which process is called a *sadhana*. *Yoga sadhana* is the exploitation of a possibility for a unitive
vision or a unitive experience.

When you move toward that by applying that
method, your present psychophysical organism with its
colorations and conditionings is not immediately available to that experience. That means that if there are
some conditions that are hostile, rigid, or not pliable,
we have to see how we can decondition them. If there
are colorations, we have to see how we can get over
them. For that we have to attempt repeatedly to erase
from the mind some conditionings and to establish
new co-ordinations, new correlations. That's called
abhyasa, or *yoga abhyasa*. In yoga we have three stages.

One is an *abhyasa*, which is meant for a *sadhana*, which is meant for a *darsana*.

We begin from the first. That is, first we make clear in our mind what we seek and then we look for the path and then we make an application of that path. If these are not clear in our mind, then we just go to the yoga class and give five dollars, and so long as we give the five dollars, the instructor will go on asking us to bend our body in so many ways. I read an advertisement in the newspaper that new classes are going to be open for yoga instruction, belly dancing, and dog training. You can take all three, and if you enroll for all three, you only have to pay fifteen dollars. That is the way in which the subject is usually treated in America.

Now, going more seriously into the subject of meditation—I call it familiarization. We are not familiar with ourselves. Making yourself more familiar with yourself, I consider a very sane approach. Jung says that everything has an unknown side and every person has an unconscious aspect. Within us there is an unconscious aspect, and with our body and the bodies outside and the people outside there is an unknown aspect. The unknown and the unconscious together make such a vast area to seek; the known and conscious is so small.

First, to be familiar with my own body, I just sit. I close my eyes and see how much I am familiar with my own body. I try to figure out where my body ends. If I touch, I know where it is, but with your eyes closed and without touching, try to find out your own body outlines. You will find that you are really getting lost. It's your own body, and yet you do not know the body outline. Somewhere in you it becomes vague. Where your body ends and where the atmosphere begins, you don't know, unless there is a cold wind. Then look for the various pressures that you feel while you sit. For the first time you experience that you are a heavy body and that you are resting on your buttocks or thighs or feet, and you feel the pressures of it. That's also very vague. To make it precise and very clear, it takes days. You try it; you'll find it takes days.

Once you settle down to this search within you, you will find that you are not only a heavy body but that this body is functioning on its own, not needing very much your giving any consent to it. If you place your hands at the belly and if you keep it like that for some time, you will find a new dialogue coming into being. Your belly will get into a dialogue with your palm. Some gentle pressures will start coming to the palm, and the palm gets into a kind of reciprocity. The palm becomes sensitive enough to find out the heaving. If you sit like that for half an hour, you will begin to realize that your hand is something wonderful. The sensitivity that is in the fingertips and the palm is a thousand times more than what we know. You will begin to rely on your palm much more than on your eyes or ears. The very touch of it will bring to you many new messages to your body.

The rhythm that is established, that is sensed by the palm of your hand and the breathing, brings your mind more and more to the rhythm of the breath you take. You see it as an up and down movement, an ascent and a descent. At first the ascent and descent are felt only between the nose and the throat. Sometimes it comes to the lungs. Then you become more sensitive and you feel how the diaphragm is involved and how it comes to the abdomen. The more you begin to penetrate into the mechanism of its movement, you find it is like two magnetic poles between which something is oscillating.

Here we introduce a little technique. The yogi or instructor asks you to locate one pole between the eyebrows and the other pole between the tip of the spine and the anus. If you contract the anus and bring a little pressure there and make the pressure move toward the tip of the spine, you get a peculiar feeling there. That is treated as one pole. That is the pole that is bringing the vital forces down. The other pole, between the eyebrows, is bringing them up. When you go more and more into that and become very familiar with it, it becomes like a vertical line. You need not look for any physiological column or any special nerve. It's a mental line. As your consciousness is directed more toward it, the unconscious elements in your organism and the unknown in your body become like a great darkness in which your consciousness is just like a candle burning. First it is only like a light that you focus in your mind for your attention. Later it becomes like a streak of light that has a kind of an aura around it. You become familiar with all those things that are participating in that movement. You get more inner light filling you. Fortunately, there are many persons who have done this and had the same kind of experiences with which your experience can be tallied to see that you are not going astray.

In this movement you find that certain reactions affect the whole body. We look at the places where these reactions occur as synergic centers.[1] There is one synergic center between the brows and one at the throat. The one at the heart is not really at the heart but where the diaphragm and the chest are separated.

[1] In Sanskrit the term for them is *chakra*. Editor.

You can find a little pit there where if you press, you get a funny feeling. Then there is a synergic center at the navel. At the genitals it can be located by contracting the muscles there to the base, and at that point, like at the lowest center, at the anus, you will get an unusual feeling. These are the six synergic centers.

As mind has a tendency to seek new interests, one of nature's devices is to satiate the senses and the mind with one experience so that they will automatically give that up and go to another. If you don't blink your eye, it won't get lubrication. If you stare at one thing, it gets tired. So you automatically look at many things. What is true of the senses is also true of the mind. We say that a modulation of consciousness comes and it is the mental experience of one unit. A modulation is like a wave. A wave cannot be kept up. A wave comes to a climax, and then it falls. It disappears and gives room for the next wave. The mind has many waves, but we now want it to remain with one modulation until we become fully familiar with whatever potential it has.

To keep that single modulation, we feed it again with the same potency so that the same wave is repeated. For this a mantra is given. This can just be any interesting or not interesting sound notation. When you repeat it, you can find that it gives you some unexpected experiences, and many are taken by that, not knowing what it is. This is particularly the case if you are running around all day, and in the evening you come home, sit there, and bring your mind between the eyebrows. Then you use any term—for example, *ram* (pronounced "răm"). Then you sit and repeat, "*Ram, ram, ram.*" You make a spiral and you make it less and less so that it converges. Surely this will put you to self-hypnosis. The monotony of the sound and the way in which you are working it into a central apex causes hypnosis—in this case very calm, very quiet.

Now you are encouraged to try it the next day. As you are now more receptive, you find it even more satisfactory. Now you start looking for lights and things. Surely you will see it. If you look for the ghost, you will see the ghost. If you look for God, you will see God. Our mind is a miracle monger and a miracle maker. It is the greatest mythmaker of the world, so whatever you want, you will get.

Now you start seeing all these experiences, but something in you is honest; you are not totally a liar. That honest mind in you is now suppressed by this fictitious mythmaking propensity of the mind. The honest mind says, "No, no, no, it's not right. So many daily functions and natural ways of expressing myself are all shelved, and instead you are sitting and saying, '*Ram, ram, ram.*' I want to reject this." The body thus builds up a resistance. Your saner mind now puts up a resistance. After reaching a peak experience, you find that you cannot go any further. For six months it was all fine, but now it is not taking you any further. You do not want to admit that it is a failure. Now you have terrible experiences, and as you do not want to go with those experiences, you have to stop. But these terrible experiences were fictitious. It's all created by the mind. If you just hang on a technique, the technique won't take you anywhere.

Now you go back. You began with a mantra. What was the purpose of the mantra? The purpose of the mantra was to keep your consciousness in the same place for enough time for you to explore deeper into it. When you said, "*Ram, ram, ram,*" the first consciousness of *ram* was very intense, and then like a wave or a ripple, it receded. You were then putting a second *ram* there, and it was more intense. Now you had two circles of *ram*, an outer circle of *ram* that is at the memory level and an inner circle of *ram* at the perceptual level. At the third repetition of *ram* you have three circles of *ram*, and the center is still very intense and it brings it to a converging point. When it comes to a converging point from where it cannot go any further, there comes the rebellion. Now the intensity becomes less and less. Thereafter it becomes so mechanical that you think of *ram*, but you also think of hamburger. However much you try to avoid that, that thought is coming. So I say, why don't you put "hamburger" now in the middle? Go on saying *ram* vocally and mentally say *hamburger*. At least you get then an interest that belongs to you. You needn't do this for a long time—only until you become familiar with it.

But before that something valuable will happen. It is sort of like taking LSD; that is, you get a kick. It changes your idea about the world, your idea about the mind, your idea about your own system. It is like somebody has given you a big kick in your bottom and suddenly everything changes. This new dimension to which you come, if you are successful, brings you closer to your inner psyche; it takes you away from your physical hangups. It has within it a novelty, a uniqueness of experience, and many unfamiliar ranges. All these are so intriguing that you want to go deeper into it. Here a mere mantra will not help you. So you now try to syncronize two things. One is the *prana* with which you began this. You used it as a kind of a hammer. Secondly, you used the mantra for the localization of the mind. Now with the hammer of *prana* and the localization of the mantra, you make a kind of an interaction. This brings in more and more of an inner opening.

Now we can say that you are very much in the world of meditation. This meditation is not the directing of any reason. It is not a thinking process, but it is rather a watching of the wonders of your own inner world opening up. And as you are watching, each step will suggest to you the next step. Here actually it is not the preceptor who is helping you. You find your preceptor as a light from within you that looks as if it wants you to go to greater and greater depth. If you are an artist, you know this. When you make a stroke with your brush, it suggests back to you what is to be the next stroke. You enter into a dialogue with the canvas. And in this dialogue there is a two-way progress in which you make a stroke, and from there a beauty opens up which suggests another beauty. When you go deeper in your mind, it is suggested to you to move in that direction; and that gives to you a greater direction. This, in short, is how we enter into the world of meditation.

I do not recommend meditation to anyone unless he shows a tendency to turn inward and make a search. Suppose a man is a devotional type. If he's a Christian, I try to help him to understand Christ as a living reality. If he is a Muslim, I try to help him see how Allah, the Absolute, is all-powerful and how in His mercy we live and how the Word of Allah came through the prophet and is to be lived and followed. If he is a Buddhist, I will never speak to him about God at all. I try to help him to analyze the aggregates and the wheel of karma and things like that. Meditation is not a panacea for all.

If there are clouds in your meditation, it is because you think that you have to *catch* meditation. You think you have to bring something to prevail on your mind so that it won't run away. I say you are doing

violence to your nature. If a thought wants to cross
your mind, allow the fellow to run around a little. There
is a story in which Jesus says, "Sparrows may fly over
your head. Allow them to. Only you don't have to allow them to make a nest in your beard." The thoughts
passing over your head are something in you like children. Don't you like children playing around on the
ground? Like that, let your thoughts play on the
ground of your mind. Watch them. They're beautiful.
They look naughty, but they're not naughty. They
are also part of your being. Love them, and when you
love them, they don't want to play games with you.
Then they will also want to sit with you and meditate.
You will never get your meditation until your thoughts
decide to meditate.

How to Meditate

The Silent World

Robert S. de Ropp

ROBERT S. DE ROPP *is a biochemist who has done research on cancer, mental illness, and the biochemistry of the brain. His books include* Drugs and the Mind *and* Science and Salvation.

THE LEGITIMATE ROAD to the fourth room of consciousness and the fifth lies through the silent world, the world of simple awareness, beyond words, beyond thoughts. Psychedelic drugs may lead the traveler into the silent world, may give him a taste of the beauties and wonders it contains, but they cannot keep him in this world. Though he takes mescaline by the spoonful, saturates his system with LSD, inhales nitrous oxide till he reels in stupor, he still cannot hope to hold the treasure of silence. Only by work, by a steady, unremitting effort, can he learn to stop the wheel of the imagination, to halt that flood of inner conversations, arguments, mere chatter, with which the roof brain, by its useless overactivity, floods the awareness from dawn to dusk.

Adapted from *The Master Game,* by Robert S. de Ropp. Copyright © 1968 by Robert S. de Ropp. Used by permission of the publisher. A Seymour Lawrence Book/Delacorte Press.

While this noise persists, no deep awareness is possible. So for one who really wishes to *practice*,[1] the first rule is very simple: *Enter the silence as often as possible; remain there for as long as possible.*

Stop thoughts!

In the quiet that follows, permit the impressions brought by each separate sense to float on the surface of a calm awareness. The eye rests on the objects of sight, not naming them, not desiring, passing no judgments. *As with sights, so with sounds.* In the healing silence that follows the stopping of thoughts, all sounds take on a new significance. Nature echoes, reverberates through a rich spectrum of tonalities formerly unperceived. There are inward sounds also, not only the almost imperceptible throb of the heart, but subtler sounds, scarcely sounds at all, originating from who knows what interactions. (The yogis have known them for centuries and call them *nadas*.) *As with sights and sounds, so with odors.* . . .

Stopping thoughts, the practice of simple awareness: these are the keys with which a man can unlock the fourth room. To one who has never tried to use this method, it might appear almost too easy. What could be simpler than to impose silence on the gibbering roof brain, which, like a badly designed radio, generates so much noise (using this term in the electronic sense) that every message is distorted?

Few disciplines, however, are more uncongenial to

[1] " . . . theory . . . can be studied in books . . . *practice* is a different matter. For this a teacher is necessary. . . . Only by finding a teacher and becoming part of the group of pupils . . . can the player find encouragement and support. He must find a teacher who is neither a fool nor a fraud and convince that teacher that the would-be pupil is worth teaching. His future development depends largely on the skill with which he performs this task." Ibid., pp. 25–26.

contemporary man than the intentional silencing of the noise machine. This gibbering mechanism ceaselessly pouring out its flood of inner conversations, arguments, schemes, and aimless chatter has come to occupy so large a place in man's awareness that he often regards it as his very self. If this noise is switched off accidentally or if he switches it off intentionally, he has an uneasy feeling of nonexistence. Contemporary man, using this term somewhat loosely to describe the mass-produced semi-automata that make up the bulk of the world's large man-swarms, fears inner silence and avoids places that induce inner silence, be they deserts or mountains or empty stretches of ocean. All inner work involves the imposing of inner silence. To enter the silence as often as possible and to remain there for as long as possible is the goal of all followers of the Way, be they yogis, Sufis, Zen Buddhists, or Christian mystics. As Arjuna said to Krishna: "The mind is restless, turbulent, powerful, and obstinate. I deem it as difficult to control as the wind."

AWARENESS AND ATTENTION

The practice of simple awareness is impossible without control of attention. Attention is to awareness as the oil in a lamp is to its flame. While there is oil in the lamp, the flame persists. Once the oil is exhausted, the flame goes out. Control of attention is the one function that man possesses that may be said to confer on him a certain amount of free will. He can "direct his attention." But his power to do this depends upon his possessing a certain kind of energy the supply of which is limited. Each day, on awakening, he has just so much of this energy, as a battery after being charged contains just so much electrical potential. His inner work each day depends on the conservation of this energy. Once it has been squandered, it is hard to replace.

A man's level of consciousness can be measured by the freedom of his attention. In the state of identification he has no "freedom to attend." *He thinks he has*, but this is one of the illusions that this state imposes. "Waking sleep," "hypnotized sleep," "walking sleep," "identification," are different names for the third room. In this state man does not really know who he is, where he is, why he is, or even whether he is—a sleepwalker. If man could be aware of his state of sleep, how eagerly, how urgently, he would struggle to awaken! For waking sleep is dangerous and dismal. Waking sleep is inner slavery and inner unrest. Endlessly men prate about freedom, and shout and demonstrate and riot and demand congressional legislation and civil rights. All in vain. The fetters are inward, the bondage is spiritual. The name of the great enslaver is Identification, and the result of his domination is "waking sleep."

Only when a person learns to withdraw from the task in hand, to maintain a certain thread of awareness that remains apart from thinking, feeling, sensing, does he begin to get the taste of the fourth state of consciousness. In this state he *is*; he exists objectively for himself as a tree exists, a table exists, a book exists. He is aware of the room in which he is sitting, of himself as one of the objects in that room, of his "inner space" and of his outer space: room, house, surroundings, planets, suns, not in specific details but as a totality, as a *presence*. In this state the self is not separate, and the attention, though directed to whatever the task in hand, is at the same time flexible and open, not rigid and narrow.

This sensing of the self as not self but merely as one of the objects of the environment removes at one stroke all fears, all tensions, all anxieties. A condition of buoyancy and ease, a delightful ataraxy, falls to the lot of one in whom such a condition has been induced. He is in harmony with Tao, the unconditioned, unnameable source of all reality.

This living in harmony with Tao, this inner freedom, is not attained without long and careful training. It is a state of physiological and psychological equipoise, seemingly effortless, but maintained by a watchfulness as real as that which enables the tightrope walker to maintain his balance high above the heads of the crowd. There is no tension in this watchfulness. It is flexible, pervasive, an invisible shield, an instrument that *catches and holds* impressions before these impressions can set the inner machinery in motion.

AWARENESS AND IMPRESSIONS

Generalized attention separated from the ego offers to one who employs it the power of choice of impressions. He who has a watchman at the gate can scrutinize all who try to enter, can receive the impressions he chooses and reject the rest. There is no other art more important than the art of receiving impressions. Man's instincts seem to give him little guidance. A cow or a horse grazing in a meadow is generally warned by instinct to avoid poisonous plants, but a man, whose impressions are just as much a food as his bread, shows no such discrimination. On the contrary, he will often *deliberately seek* poisonous impressions, compelled by some perverse impulse to degrade his own inner life, already sufficiently polluted. A degenerate "entertainment" industry does not hesitate to take advantage of this perverse taste, pouring out through all its various channels a stream of more or less pathological material that readers, viewers, and listeners eagerly absorb into their psyches.

Poise, balance, inner harmony, the "creation of an island that no flood can immerse"[2]—all this can be achieved by one who has learned to handle his impressions. Between the moment when an impression strikes and the reaction to that impression elapses a time so short it can hardly be measured by man's ordinary awareness. Yet much may depend on what happens in that brief interval.

Accept or reject[3]—this is the basis of the inner work that leads to the genesis of a truly free being. A man's health, as well as his inner development and level of being, depends just as much on how his impressions are metabolized as on how his food is metabolized. The way in which impressions are metabolized depends on the level of attention and on the *quality* of that attention. This is why, in the fourth state of consciousness, impressions take on such extraordinary richness, as if seen for the first time. The simplest objects become enhaloed with all sorts of hidden meanings that were previously not noticed.[4] It may occur often in children and cease to happen later. It may be brought about by certain psychedelics. But for the majority of people, no other way is available but to begin work on the control of attention, preventing it from wandering,

[2] The Dhammapada. Irving Babbit translation.

[3] The New Testament. "But let your response be 'yea' or 'nay'; for whatsoever is more cometh of evil."

[4]   To see a world in a grain of sand,
        And a heaven in a wild flower;
        Hold infinity in the palm of your hand
        And eternity in an hour.

                              —William Blake

holding it as one holds water in a brimming bowl, using it to "capture" impressions, to accept and digest those that nourish and to reject those that poison.

CONSERVATION OF AWARENESS

Nothing that man possesses is more precious than his awareness. It is a material entity, like muscular energy, and its level fluctuates during the day. It lies within a man's power to squander the vital resource or to conserve it. There are creative activities and destructive activities. There are activities that enrich the doer. There are activities that serve to inflate the ego, that involve falsehoods and depend on the propagation of big or little lies. There are activities (they constitute a huge and hideous industry) that prostitute the fruits of scientific discovery for purposes of mass destruction. There are activities that funnel funds and resources into semi-imbecile projects and feats of stratospheric jugglery only fit to arouse the wonder of children and fools.

KNOW WHAT YOU ARE DOING AND WHY

In large activities, in small activities, set definite limits. Strive all the while to keep the inner silence, to practice simple awareness, to receive impressions simply and directly. Every activity offers profound insights concerning the interplay of forces, the qualities of materials. Similarly the activity, performed with the right degree of double awareness, illuminates the inner workings of the organism, revealing to the objective observer those subtle rhythms of tension and relaxation that give to the simplest act a smoothness and flow reminiscent of musical harmony or the gestures of a dancer. Remember only a beautiful saying of Yun-men as recorded by Alan Watts in *The Way of Zen*: "In walking, just walk, in sitting, just sit. Above all, don't wobble."

RESTORING LOST BALANCE

The above procedures all relate to maintaining the state of simple awareness, of inner silence. The state can be compared to balance, the "vital balance" that enables a man to control his reactions to impressions instead of being blown about like a feather in the wind. But the reader will rightly insist that maintaining this balance is a difficult art, one learned only by long practice. So what is one to do who has lost his balance? —is "upset"? His thoughts and feelings are in turmoil. His entire awareness is occupied with stormy thoughts, accusations of others, justification of himself, expostulations and recriminations. These go on and on with maddening persistence, like a phrase repeated by a phonograph with its needle caught in a groove. With a storm raging in the mind, he can no more engage in the practice of simple awareness than can the captain of a ship being battered by a hurricane engage in writing sonnets.

Transfer the energy from the destructive process into a creative process. This is most readily accomplished by undertaking some physical task, the more vigorous the better. Chop firewood, dig the garden, dance the gopak, climb the Sierras. But the physical outlet is often not available. This leaves two other procedures either of which can serve to drain the energy from its destructive cycle. The first of these is *repetition*; the second is *visualization*. Both practices serve the same end; they provide the agitated mind with a firm support to which it can cling as a shipwrecked sailor clings to a floating spar. *It is not a substitute for the practice of simple awareness; it is a temporary expedient, to be used in emergencies.*

Repetition involves some phrase or a series of sentences that is placed so forcibly in the focus of attention that it drives out all other material. In the Judeo-Christian tradition repetition centers around a prayer. In the Hindu-Buddhist tradition it centers around a mantra. A mantra differs from a prayer in being often only a sound, perhaps a single syllable, like the syllables *aum* or *hum*.[5] A prayer consists of a sentence or several sentences. There are very few real prayers. Real prayers always have the same aim: to lead the one who prays out of the third room into the fourth. The simplest of prayers, and from the standpoint of repetition the most effective, consists of three words: "God help me." It makes no difference actually whether the person using this prayer "believes in God," whatever this hackneyed phrase may mean. The important thing is that by relating the petty ego struggling in its morass of self-pity, indignation, injured dignity, etc., to another entity far greater than itself, a sense of proportion is restored. Furthermore, by concentrating the attention on the repetition of the syllables, *accompanied by rhythmic and directed breathing*, he who repeats the prayer drains away energy from the destructive, repetitive inner noise. Thus, the useless drain of vital energy is halted, the vicious circle is broken, and the

[5] Or the Rinzai Zen *mu* or the Soto Zen (Reirin Yamada's) *un(shu)*, or the mantras of Maharishi Mahesh Yogi's Transcendental Meditation (TM) or even the single syllables "Lord" or "love," from the fifteenth-century anonymous *Cloud of Unknowing.*

awareness shifted from a very narrow preoccupation to a wider horizon.

The Buddhist mantra *Aum mane padme hum*[6] can also be used as a basis for repetition by those who prefer "Buddhist" forms to "Christian" ones. In a more simplified form this mantra has only three sounds, *aum, ah, hum*, the symbols visualized as white, red, and blue, respectively. This mantra is the basis of mantric breathing described in Tibetan literature, the *hum* corresponding to the in breath, the *ah* to the suspension when breath is held locked in the body, and the *aum* to the out breath.

Visualization, the second method of silencing the restless mind, is based on various symbols or diagrams which, in the Western tradition, are called arcana and in the Hindu tradition *yantra*. Arcana of various kinds have long been associated in the West with magic, the "calling up of spirits," and the release of "higher forces" (whatever this may mean). About this, a good deal of nonsense has been spoken and written. Transformation only occurs after long practice, when the arcana come to life and begin to move and interact. Until they do so, they remain merely pictures and diagrams.

Exactly the same thing is true of the Eastern *yantra*. A *yantra* may be a picture of some god or a diagram such as a *mandala*. A properly drawn *mandala* is a book in itself containing a great deal of information, but he who would read the symbols must learn the language.[7]

[6] Or the Nembutsu *Namu amida bu*, of Shin Buddhism, or Sokagakai's *Namyo ho renge Kyo*, of Nichiren Buddhism.

[7] The preoccupation of C. G. Jung with *mandalas* has led to widespread misunderstanding of these *yantras* in the West. "In Indian or Tibetan spiritual practices, they are instruments for concentrating the mind, which has to pass beyond them" (Hans Jacobs).

Arcana or *yantra* can be used to provide a fixed point for the disturbed mind, the diagram or picture being visualized and held in the field of awareness. The effort of holding it little by little drains energy from the destructive mental process and attaches it to a creative process, re-establishing the sense of proportion and enabling the student to laugh at his egotistical preoccupations which, in the presence of the larger concepts, appear trivial indeed. After the storm has subsided, he can return again to the silent world and to the practice of simple awareness, which, slowly but surely, will bring him to the fourth room and finally to the fifth.

A Meditation on Meditation

Charles C. Wise, Jr.

CHARLES C. WISE, JR., *has held various legal and administrative positions in the United States government since 1933. At present, he is department counsel in the office of the Secretary of Defense. He is the author of two books,* Windows on the Passion *and most recently,* Windows on the Master.

THERE IS CIRCULATING CURRENTLY a mass of material concerning "meditation," "entering the silence," etc. It shows a very great deal of confusion as to what meditation really is, what it does, whether and how it differs from prayer, whether it can be done in groups or must be done alone, and whether certain positions, breathing techniques, or environmental elements are essential to its success. Many seem to promise prompt results—a sort of instant cosmic consciousness—without sustained effort or the detriment of using drugs. This article is a sincere effort to bring order out of esoteric chaos and to offer encouragement to those

Reprinted from *Spiritual Frontiers* 3, no. 4 (Autumn 1971), by permission of Spiritual Frontiers Fellowship, 800 Custer Avenue, Evanston, Illinois 60202.

serious seekers embarked on the eternal adventure and
joyously journeying on the endless quest.[1]

What is meditation? A good short course in its essentials was given the author many years ago. Age and
arthritis then kept Uncle Henry out of the fiel ls, but he
still occupied his cottage and shared in the produce of
the farm. All summer long, on every sunny day, he
could be seen rocking on his porch. Once I asked him,
"Uncle Henry, what do you do in that chair all day?"
Thoughtfully he replied, "Mist' Charles, sometimes I
sits and thinks, an' sometimes I jes' sits." Exactly! And
in that order! That's meditation! Work hard; relax, and
think to the limits of thought; then relax unthinking,
and allow the Infinite to lift your understanding toward His.

Although that little parable contains the essentials
of this article, it is too skeletal for comprehension until
fleshed out with the various percepts, concepts, pre-
cepts, and excepts that follow.

What Meditation Is Not

Let us begin our guided meditation into the process
itself by considering some whats that meditation is

[1] I can recommend unreservedly only two of the many books
readily available. The best simple textbook on the what, how,
and why of meditation is E. V. Ingraham's *Meditation in the
Silence*, first published in 1922 and since then regularly obtain-
able from the Unity School of Christianity, Unity Village, Mis-
souri 64063. It is superb, not only for what it contains, but for
the foolishness it omits. More deeply analytical is Dr. Martin
Israel's *An Approach to Mysticism*, six lectures delivered at the
College of Psychic Science in London in 1968 and published
jointly by the College and the Churches' Fellowship for Psychical and Spiritual Studies. His little book, so big in scope, can
be obtained by writing to the Fellowship, 5/6 Denison House,
Vauxhill Bridge Road, London S.W. 1, England.

not. In this connection, James Martineau, a British theologian whose long life spanned all but five years of the nineteenth century, has given us this most helpful and beautiful statement:

> There is an act of the mind, natural to the earnest and the wise, impossible only to the sensual and the fool, healthful to all who are sincere, which has small place in modern usage and which few can distinguish from vacuity. Those who knew what it was called it *meditation*. It is not *Reading*, in which we apprehend the thoughts of others. It is not *Study*, in which we strive to master the known and prevail over it till it lies in order beneath our feet. It is not *Deliberation*, which reckons up the forces which surround our individual lot and projects accordingly the expedient on the right. It is not *Self-scrutiny*, which by itself is only shrewdness. Its view is not personal and particular, but universal and immense. It brings not an intense self-consciousness and spiritual egotism, but almost a renunciation of individuality. It gives us no matter for criticism and doubt, but everything for wonder and love. It furnishes immediate perception of things divine, eye to eye with the saints, spirit to spirit with God, peace to peace with heaven.
>
> In thus being alone with the truth of things and passing from shows and shadows into communion with the Everlasting One, there is nothing at all impossible and out of reach.
>
> Let any man go into the Silence; strip himself of all pretense and selfishness and sensuality and sluggishness of soul; lift off thought after thought, passion after passion till he reaches the inmost depths of all, and it will be strange if he does not feel the Eternal Presence close upon his soul—if he does not say, "O Lord, art Thou ever near as this and have I not known Thee?"

In a general reading (Reading 281-41) given for the Association for Research and Enlightenment on June

15, 1939, Edgar Cayce stated: "It [meditation] is not *musing*, not *daydreaming*; but as ye find your bodies made up of the physical, mental, and spiritual, it is the attuning of the mental body and the physical body to its spiritual source."

Meditation is not *emptying the mind*. In this connection, Jesus' cryptic Parable of the Displaced Demon (Matt. 12:43–45; Luke 11:24–26) speaks its warning. After the evil spirit was cast out, it found no new home. So it returned to the mind it had left. Finding it empty, it moved back with seven other devils more evil than it, and the man was worse off than in the beginning. Certainly this parable means that you cannot break an evil habit merely by getting rid of it; you must fill its place with the wholesome and constructive or there will be a relapse. But it also means that, if you just sit passively with your bare mind hanging out, you are inviting possession by any peripatetic evil spirit which happens to be around. This is the great danger of the Ouija board and of automatic writing, and is why a successful trance medium always has a strong control standing guard. Meditation must be centered on *something*. And it is well to begin with a prayer invoking divine protection.

Is Meditation a Form of Prayer?

The Cayce reading cited above presents these provocative sentences: "In the mind of many, there is little or no difference between meditation and prayer. And there are many [others?] gathered here who, through their studies of various forms, have very definite ideas as to meditation and prayer." So it continues today!

Clearly, Edgar Cayce opts for a difference:

Prayer is the concerted effort of the physical consciousness to become attuned to the consciousness of the Creator, either collectively or individually. *Meditation* is emptying self of all that hinders from the creative forces rising along the natural channels of the physical man. . . . As we give out, so does the whole of man—physically and mentally—become depleted. Yet . . . entering into the silence in meditation . . . we may receive that strength and power that fits each individual, each soul, for a greater activity in this material world.

[In meditation] ye are seeking to know the will or activity of the Creative Forces; for ye are raising in meditation actual creation taking place within the inner self!

There is an idea here, struggling to be expressed. Attempting to clarify this, a thoughtful disciple of Cayce suggests the following:

Prayer: the concerted effort of our physical consciousness to become attuned with the Consciousness of the Creator. Talking to God; out-pouring of the soul.

Meditation: attuning our mental and physical bodies to their spiritual source, seeking to know our relationship with God. God talking to us; in-pouring of the Holy Spirit.

Prayer is the question, meditation is the answer.

This is interesting, whether or not it is true or correctly reflects Cayce. Note the implication that meditation is masculine and prayer is feminine, and recall the yin and yang principles of Chinese classical philosophy. There is some basis for this. Frances Banks[2] in *Four Studies in Mysticism* (Churches' Fellowship for

2 Frances Banks as a discarnate provided the report from beyond the grave that constitutes the *Testimony of Light* (Churches' Fellowship for Psychical and Spiritual Studies, 1969), a book that no seeker of esoteric truth should miss.

Psychical and Spiritual Studies, 1967) contrasts St. John of the Cross with St. Teresa of Avila in somewhat this way.

I believe a distinction between meditation and prayer is valid and helpful. But rather than put it on the basis of the direction in which communication is moving, I prefer to seek it on the basis of a difference in aim or emphasis. *Meditation* is a search for the Creator (the Father), a search that begins in the mind and seeks knowledge (relationships), a search that culminates in revelation or cosmic consciousness, contact with the mind of God. *Prayer* is a search for the Comforter (the Holy Spirit), a search that begins in the soul with emotions of longing and yearning, seeks the response of a person, and finds its culmination in union with the Infinite, the spiritual orgasm of ecstasy (see the picture of Bernini's statue of St. Teresa in Kenneth Clarke's *Civilization*). Upon return to the world after the withdrawal, meditation issues in action as invention, discovery, and creativity; prayer as love, service, and sacrifice. Meditation is available to the agnostic and the unbeliever; Prayer is dependent upon faith in God. In either, a blind faith in established authority of a church, a book (Bible), or a principle (science) terminates growth and abandons the quest in fear or fatigue. Both meditation and prayer are subsumed under the more comprehensive category *mysticism*. Buddha meditating under the banyan tree received illumination; Jesus fasting in the wilderness found God. Buddha is the way of meditation; Christ, the way of prayer.

There is little doubt that, at the *highest* levels, the processes tend to lose their differences and merge into one. Part of this is due to inadequate terminology. The culmination of both is an ineffable experience, and it is not strange that efforts to express the inexpressible (to "unscrew the inscrutable"), inevitably using the same inadequate words, convey impressions that often are indistinguishable. But all mysticism ultimately leads to God. The way of meditation must modify selfish indifference by learning to care. The way of prayer must curb the impulse to interfere by helping before it understands or is asked, and must recognize the rights of others to determine their own paths and rates of growth.

I cannot leave this section without giving you a taste of the exquisite insight and accuracy of Dr. Martin Israel. This is out of context, and somewhat condensed, but the flavor is conveyed:

THE APPROACH TO GOD: PRAYER AND MEDITATION

In man's willed ascent to the Godhead two techniques are pre-eminent: prayer and meditation. Prayer is the way of petition in which the emotion of personal devotion dominates, while meditation is the way of concentration in which the will to comprehend leads. Prayer is the way of the heart (emotion) while meditation is the way of the head (intellect). When both are carried to their ultimate summation both emotion and reason are transcended by intuitional understanding, which is the outcome of mystical illumination.

Prayer starts as a heart-to-heart pleading and petition with that greater than the self, either in respect of one's own wishes and demands (petitionary prayer) or with regard to the well-being of others (intercessory prayer). . . . The petition may or may not be answered satisfactorily in terms of the person's own limited point of view, but, as the techniques of approach and invocation are proceeded with, a greater devotion develops between the individual and the personal God. In the most highly developed people . . . petition and intercession are transcended in a union of lover and beloved that embraces all categories of experience. This is mystical prayer (I and the Father are one in love), and it finds its summation in the prayer of thanksgiving, in which one's own life is poured out in joy to the whole created universe as an offering in love to God. . . .

Meditation . . . is to be seen as a technique of mind-training whereby the constantly flowing kaleidoscopic juxtaposition of ideas and thoughts (the "mind stream" of William James) is controlled and subdued. This is achieved by concentrating on one theme or subject to the exclusion of all else. . . . As progress is made the person . . . becomes more united with the theme, until it forms a part of his own consciousness. . . . In the highest stage, which is called contemplation, both the person and the subject have merged into that reality which is of mystical extent. . . .

It is evident that the objective of both prayer and meditation is the transcendence of the limited consciousness of the person by an all-pervading consciousness of total reality. . . .

In the properly blended person, prayer and meditation play their full part in the spiritual life. . . . The shortcoming of meditation is a selfish detachment from the world of suffering and the entry into a private world of release and refreshment. Indeed, the best meditation is meditation on behalf of others which merges imperceptibly into intercessory prayer. On the other hand, prayer can be merely a selfish outpouring of personal craving. It has to be elevated to a transpersonal level by commitment to the world.[3]

When one contemplates or meditates upon Jesus Christ, there is found the idea or ideal (Christ) in the person (Jesus), and meditation and prayer become one.

[3] Israel, op. cit. pp. 33–36.

MEDITATION DEFINED

Meditation is a mental discipline in which relationships are revealed. It is a process of pattern-recognition in which the mind is raised above the particulars to receive universals which give coherence to the particulars.

True meditation consists in allowing the mind to make unlimited flights of speculation regarding the nature of the mind of God, the power of this Mind, the love of this Mind, the wisdom contained in this Mind, the substance that comes from this Mind and out of which all things are formed, the instant availability of all the elements of this Mind to the individual who is open and receptive to it.[4]

CAN MEDITATION BE TAUGHT?

Meditation is a growth process. It is not a specific technique producing guaranteed results. It cannot be taught with assurance or learned infallibly. It is acquired slowly and haltingly, and then only where there is a persistent search motivated by disciplined desire. How any individual can best progress in it is not a matter of dogmatic rule and varies widely from person to person. The best that can be done is to indicate in the most general terms the elements involved and to let each individual find his own way by trial and error. No guru should be trusted utterly; let God be your guru. Jesus said: "Call no man your Father, but God only; and be not called 'teacher' or 'master,' for each man has both in the in-dwelling Christ" (Matt. 23: 8–10).

[4] Ingraham, op. cit. p. 22.

A major reason that meditation cannot be taught is that no one knows *how* to do it. Not all who do things know *how* they do them; one must understand how, to *teach*. Even those very successful, whose efforts are crowned with the most penetrating insights, do not know what they did right to trigger the revelation. It is not under the meditator's control, and he cannot turn it on and off at will. Socrates' *daemon* visited him as it willed; he did not control it.

Is meditation man's act, God's act, or both? Is it something that either can avoid? There is, in successful meditation, an outside element or variable that can be called *divine grace*. Is the insight gained God's gift, or man's grasp, or a flash from each that meets as in the lightning bolt? We cannot know, but we who meditate sense it as an influx from the Other. The picture that springs into consciousness, the reconciling ideas, does not come from us. We gain by grace. The Lord giveth and the Lord withholdeth; blessed be the name of the Lord. Though one may and must seek with all application and diligence, the answer does not yield automatically to effort. Desire for gain is not the key; one must give one's self utterly in love to the area of knowledge, interest, or art—or to God—in order to receive. We lose by grasping, and gain by letting go.

ELEMENTS OF MEDITATION

The child asks: "Why, Daddy?" The purpose of meditation is to understand, to obtain valid information from extrasensory sources. The practice awakens the intuitional activities of the mental life. Intuition, inspiration, creativity, illumination, revelation, all are products of the process at various levels. These are never vouchsafed to the uninterested or the unprepared. The elements listed below all play their part to some extent in the meditation process:

A. *Attention.* A mule-skinner teaching army recruits how to train mules began by batting the mule between the eyes with a two-by-four. He explained: "The first and most important thing is to get the mule's attention." So it is with us. Meditation begins when something captures our attention. We invest interest and time in it; we care enough to desire to know more. Attention is the mind's attitude of devotion.

B. *Concentration.* Life progresses by the selection among alternatives, a narrowing by specialization. When our attention is caught by one area, we become determined to find out its why. The attention is concentrated by the will so that it ceases to flit hither and yon, becomes fixed for periods of increasing duration upon the matter in mind, and no longer reacts restlessly to incident and casual stimuli. The conscious mind is made obedient to the self.

This is the period of *preparation.* By reading, studying, and questioning, one learns most or all that experience knows concerning the subject of interest. The limits of conscious thought on the subject are reached.

C. *Detachment.* It is only at this point that meditation as such begins. At this stage, the self has invested heavily in the area of interest. Unaided striving has gone as far as it can. Only something from outside the conscious mind, an influx from the Other, can advance matters further.

Now the level of thinking must be raised from the concrete to the intuitional. The point of view must shift from the ego to the impersonal. Truth must be sought now for itself alone and not as a means of selfish gain. This process requires *detachment, impersonality,* and *openness.* This is the *suspension of judg-*

ment (the temporary suppression of the critical faculty) that forms the basis of much of Krishnamurti's teaching, the setting aside of all preconceptions and biases, to let the subject speak its truth to you unimpeded by you and your hangups.

Concentrating impersonally on the problem area, the conscious mind can then be brought to review all relevant material with detachment: its history in the past, its present importance for the self and others, and its possibilities for the future. This is very important for two purposes: (1) to state the problem fully and truly to the superconscious, and (2) to verbalize and express the insights received back.

Then the higher self should be sought with the intent to reach a deeper level of understanding. The mind is not made blank, but consciousness *rests* without agitation in a broad view of the whole area, lifting the problem into the silence of wordless cogitation. "Be still, and know." Restless striving has ceased. The truth exists; it can be known. The mind waits for further enlightenment from Universal Mind to make the truth clear. At lower levels, this often is called "putting it on the back of the stove."

Thomas Alva Edison was not a trained scientific researcher. But deafness aided his concentration, he learned how to ask meaningful questions, and answers seemed to come to him out of the blue. Dr. George Washington Carver spoke (in substance) to God: "Father, there is much to know and my capacity is small. I do not ask to understand everything; just tell me everything there is to know about the humble peanut." These are examples of true meditators—intuitional researchers—and the many patents granted both men attest to its potency as a medium of discovery.

D. *Illumination* (*Revelation*). Sometimes there is

a flash of illumination—a new view, clear in all of its ramifications. More often, not. Hang on to whatever comes and keep listening. Often the thought requires time to express itself, comes in driblets, or expands gradually. Many meditations often are needed to clarify. Sometimes nothing happens—there is dead silence. Often this means a charge is being built up for a flash of more than usual voltage. Wait with patience and humility, and check the self for sin (wrong attitude). One must be open to the infinite undistracted by the world. We are rewarded with truth only when we have yielded in love of truth all *striving* and *assertiveness*.

The results may not come in the meditation itself. Often the answer is discovered in the consciousness in the morning after sleep. Or it pops into the mind at night when just drifting off. All dedicated meditators know the need for the bedside tablet and pencil. Near sleep there is the letting go—the detachment—needed for reversing the flow. The results may even come at some awkward moment when you desperately desire to do something else. Paul was knocked off a horse. Martin Luther tells us he was on the toilet.

E. *Contemplation.* After the mind has been lifted repeatedly to the knowing beyond thought, in rare cases it becomes possible to maintain contact with infinite mind in a thoughtless (nonspecific) understanding, one of the meanings of that which is called cosmic consciousness. Little that is meaningful can be written concerning this. When the self is ready for transcendence, it will not need help from this level or lack it from the next.

In most of the books on meditation I have read, the reader is given specific instructions on body posture, breathing, mind techniques, and environmental dispositions (or is told that such instructions will be furnished if you subscribe to and pay for the advanced course). Many persons believe firmly in the necessity for the lotus position, the intoning of sacred mantras, standing on the head in a corner, deep-breathing in at one specified orifice and out another, etc. There is no convincing evidence that yoga, for example, is more conducive to successful *meaningful* meditation than is any other discipline directed toward concentration which is persisted in. Excessive emphasis on the body and body control does not notably free the mind for selfless thought.

I was once given the following instruction sheet, which was recommended if I aspired to achieve meaningful meditation:

I. *How to relax the physical body*

Keep feet flat on the floor (if wearing heels you should take them off).

Wear comfortable clothing, nothing that may feel tight (women should forget about wearing a girdle).

Try to keep your spine as straight as you can.

Rest your arms in your lap if your chair has no armrests. Don't hold hands together.

Begin with the small parts of the body and send thoughts to each one, telling them to completely relax. Try to start from top and go to bottom. The head and mouth area will be harder to relax because they are usually the most active. You may have to return to these parts several times and order them to relax.

Keep mouth open and let your jaw drop.

Don't worry if you fall asleep.

Don't force any muscle strain.

II. *Rhythmic breathing*

Air should go into diaphragm, not stomach.

Breath in through the nose.

Let air go into diaphragm and expand your diaphragm.

Hold it for a while (don't force yourself to hold it for any length of time).

Then exhale through the mouth. This is why your mouth should be left open.

Let all the air as possible come out. Don't worry if you make a little noise.

Do this rhythmic breathing just to the point where you start feeling the physical relaxation taking over your body. You will know if you have gone too far when you feel dizzy.

You may find yourself getting dizzy for the first couple times. Let yourself breathe normal for a while, then try again.

This may take three to six months. Don't try to push it. Go slow and take your time.

III. *Experiences*

We aren't trying to have psychic experiences; we want to learn spiritually.

Try fixing your mind on just one thing, like a cross, or repeat over and over again the word "God" or "Christ" or something on this order. Something very simple.

Sometimes you may never remember if you experienced anything.

When you are able to visualize this very easily, you will leave this and will experience things. You are now open to anything.

However well intentioned, and although it actually may have worked for some, this is sheer drivel. How loose should you get? How can you be loose with a straight spine? Why must both feet be on the floor and the hands not touching? (The Buddha's favorite position violates both!) Can't some of the air be permitted to go into the lungs and not just the diaphragm? If you faithfully follow the above, the last sentence quoted will certainly be true, but I will wager (as a good Methodist) that you are more likely to experience the jimjams than effective meditation. Some searchers lack a saving sense of humor!

Perhaps a comment should be made here on the cited tendency to go to sleep. I do not believe it is all right; St. Morpheus is no more the patron saint of meditation than is St. Vitus. One sleeps only when (1) he is tired or (2) he is bored. Prayer before meditation is good preparation. Ask God to "quicken" you. Realize his power to activate as he fills your life. And be *interested* in what Infinite Mind is going to reveal.

Edgar Cayce recommends as *one way* ("not the only one, to be sure") some tricky breathing and incantation, but he is not led astray and keeps his mind on essential things: "First *cleanse* the room; cleanse the body; cleanse the surroundings, in thought, in act! Approach not the inner man, or the inner self, with a grudge or unkind thought held against *any* man! or do so to thine own undoing sooner or later!"

The following is a recommended exercise in mind-training (not by Cayce):

> Visualize a candle burning, or look at one if you wish. Center yourself in the light. Then imagine this light being brought into your heart. Imagine the flame getting brighter and brighter and filling you, shining up through you, through your whole body. Now imagine it shining down through you. Your whole body is alight and aglow. Think of another person filled with light. See the whole room filled with light. See the walls and

the room filled to overflowing and the light overflowing into the streets. See the city filled with light, now the world, now the universe.

Götterdämmerung! A pyromaniac! Careful now, don't make an ash of yourself!

The problem here is that nobody really knows exactly what it was he did right that got results. Probably it wasn't what he did at all: God touched him. But he tries to retrace all of the empty motions that preceded contact in hopes of hitting it again. He may. Then he sets up to teach, prescribing the magic ritual as the means to the living process. Without the spirit, it is meaningless.

All religious rituals were originally techniques for meditation that once worked, and may still for some. At the Last Supper, Jesus said to the disciples (paraphrased): "Whenever you eat or drink, think of me." It was a powerful reminder and held their attention on him. Now, organized into sacredness as the Eucharist, fought over as to how it actually works (transsubstantiation), and often debased into blatant magic, it still works for many and is a priceless aid to meditation for some.

Any technique that works for you is fine—for you. *No technique is essential.* Few are truly helpful. Most may be harmful, at least to the extent of distracting attention to the nonessentials. Some may be actively dangerous.

The Buddha sought the truth by asceticism. He failed. He ceased austerities, bathed, ate a full meal (at which his disciples deserted him), and seated himself comfortably in the shade of a banyan tree. Illumination came to him. It might not have without the prior discipline, but the discipline was not the *cause*.

Saul of Tarsus was horsing after Christians when he got his. Wesley must have done most of his meditating on horseback also—when else! Even I had a major experience of insight on a Capital Transit bus. But I resist the urge to universalize from these and proclaim that one must be on the move in order to meditate. My one rule for you is this: Get comfortable so your body does not demand your attention or disturb, and get on with what it is you want to know. Be conscious to truth and unconscious to all else. And expect something to happen.

In the Foreword to *Meditation in the Silence*, Henry Ward Beecher is quoted as saying:

A man has a right to go to God by any way which is true to him. If you can think it out, that is your privilege. If you can feel it out, that is your privilege. One thing is certain: The child has a right to nestle in his father's bosom, whether he climb there upon his knee or by the chair by the side of him; any way, so that it is his father. Wherever you have seen God pass, mark it, and go and sit in that window again.

Finally, let me quote a meditation that is very meaningful to me by Frank C. Tribbe:[5]

Let us attempt this rationale by imagining the *reverse* of what might have been the original story of creation. Suppose that the various stars and stellar bodies in the heavens are now beginning, one by one, to disintegrate and blink out. Never mind how many billions of them there are, just suppose that one by one they dissolve into nothingness as you watch them. Suppose that the number of them gets down to just the bodies of our solar system, so that the only "lights" left in the heavens are our sun, plus Pluto, Neptune, Uranus, Saturn, Ju-

[5] See "A Led Meditation on the Lord's Prayer," p. 159 of this volume. *Editor.*

piter, Mars, Venus, Mercury, Earth, and the moons of each. Then suppose that these, too, begin to "go out," one by one. So long as we have Mars and Venus in existence, we people on earth would still know "where we are," astronomically; we'd locate our position in the cosmos by saying we are between Mars and Venus. Then suppose the day came when Mars "went out"; we could only say that we are on the periphery of Venus. When Venus went next, we'd be a sort of planetary moon revolving about the sun. And then one day, let's imagine the sun "went out." Here we'd be, human beings living on a sphere in the cold and utter darkness, with nothing anywhere to mark our position, and no incandescence except what we were still able to manufacture artificially. But where would we be—as to location? Without landmarks or points of reference, we'd be *nowhere*. Now suppose that all the people on this inky-black earth began to die one by one, at an accelerated pace, and with no births to replace them—till everyone is gone but you! Your own consciousness and body have persisted, but you have no other being with which to compare or evaluate yourself—no one to talk with or give you companionship. Then, quickly following this discovery of aloneness, you sense that the very planet beneath your feet is beginning to disintegrate, becoming porous, and then gossamer-like—then vaporous and etheric—and you finally sense that there is absolutely nothing beneath your feet. There you are, suspended, without feeling, but deathless, and with the knowledge that there is not another soul in the universe but you. Finally, in the last stage, you notice that your organic body is vaporizing, leaving only your self-aware mind in a complete cosmic void. Without matter, or companions, you would be only a self-aware condition of consciousness, and the only happening would be your thought processes. You would be a self-conscious Spirit —in the situation of God "in the beginning."

Our mortal imaginations may not be capable of reversing the process, to "visualize" the acts of that Mind/ Spirit by which thoughts are sent forth, actuating ether to make recognizable thought-forms that will jell into "matter." However, *this* exercise may—for logical minds conditioned in a three-dimensional material world—assist us, to a limited extent, in conceptualizing Abstract Consciousness.

GROUP MEDITATION

Some who are greatly gifted in personal meditation deny that group meditation is possible. I think that they are wrong. They know that what they have done can be done because they have done it, but they do not know that the other cannot be done merely because they have not done it yet and deem it inconsistent with what they know. Listen carefully when people tell you something they have done, seen, or known firsthand, but you need pay little heed when they explain the "impossibilities" of things never by them attempted.

The Quaker experience suggests that group silence sensitizes the social conscience. I know that prayer and study groups are fruitful. But how does a group meditation work?

Let us draw analogy from the related area of prayer. Jesus regularly withdrew to pray, and discarded his precious privacy at such times on only a few notable occasions (transfiguration, Jairus' daughter, and Gethsemane come to mind). Yet when asked by the disciples to teach them how to pray, he gave them a group prayer, and he promised that wherever two or three were gathered together in his name he would add the power of His spirit to their purposes. There is no doubt that people were (and still are) spiritually transformed in revival experiences. Let us not be blinded by the carping of the stiff-necked. Pentecost was a particularly potent example. Not all present usually reach conversion, but most may be benefited. The small groups and circles of Methodism were its power (now sadly waning). Group prayer has great power to heal.

There are difficulties, and there are benefits, in meditation used by a group of suitable people. Not all persons *can* accept guidance in meditation, and those who cannot are advised not to try. In private meditation, one can set his own pace, select the subject, and determine the purpose sought. In groups, the individual's preferences are subordinated to the group's rules, needs, and goals. In a group that knows togetherness (really united by ties of mutual love), the group consciousness supports personal effort, and more effective work can be done in the way of contacting and distributing useful influences. Regular attendance is important.

To be effective, group meditation needs guidance and often leadership. Ideally, a *sermon* is a guided meditation. In general, more formal material (ritual) is required, and usually one member is delegated to invoke the group spirit and to sound an affirmative note of aspiration and dedication. Without direction, the group consciousness may not form, or individual or group hysteria may take over. Long silences are not advisable; they may sharpen psychic perceptions but can be dangerous.

Over and above the guided type of group meditation, persons accustomed to individual meditation can meet together as a group for unstructured sessions. I do not find that an aggregate of individuals, each going his own separate mental way (however lovely and

kindly these all may be), constitutes a group meditation. Nor, in such circumstances, am I conscious of a
heightened personal awareness (although others have
claimed to be). Few group experiences of illumination
or ecstasy have been recorded as taking place in the
reading rooms of public libraries.

However, if they meet to dwell on a common subject, it may well be otherwise. In listening consciously
but quietly to music, there can be a sort of coupling
of the psychic batteries so that each individual's awareness is heightened and probes more deeply into the
darkness of the unknown. The Spirit of God (or perhaps of St. Cecilia) seems to ride the thought waves.
From the group's concentrated attention, each listener
draws a deeper understanding of new or difficult music
than he could have done alone. If it works for nonverbal music, it should assist conceptual thought.
This is a good area for experimentation. Perhaps with
all meditating on a particular nonrepresentational picture or a sacred art object—?

Few may know that there is in the Pentagon a meditation room. It is a haven of silence and an invitation
for those seeking answers of the spirit. It is much used.
The author visits it often, and some of the ideas in this
article may have been apprehended there. In this connection, it is interesting that it contains two rooms;
as one enters a sign directs solo meditators to the right
and group meditators to the left. Appropriately, the
chairs in the room to the right are the more comfortable.

COLORING AND TESTING

Sad as this may seem, the insights or illuminations
that result from meditation must not be accepted

blindly as truth. Meditation opens the mind to a flight of fancy, and all results require *testing* and *ordering* by your conscious mind. Not everything that pops into consciousness in meditation is from God or is necessarily true. It may be the voice of delusion, the devil, or your own disturbed subconscious desires.

Meditation invites response from beyond the conscious mind. Many disturbing ideas and impulses, banished from the consciousness, are repressed into the subconscious where they seek expression in ways that fool the censor at the threshold of consciousness. Some attractive or convincing ideas may prove to be but dredgings surfaced from a stirring up of the cesspool of the subconscious.

It is difficult for the individual himself, and even for others, to distinguish between revelation and the hallucinations and delusions of paranoid schizophrenia (e.g., Hitler). Most self-proclaimed messiahs have been mad. Demon possession, often misdiagnosed as schizophrenia, is also possible.

Even when the *message* is valid, *reception* may be faulty. Our scope of understanding is limited to what we already know. Illumination reveals new *relationships*, unifying concepts, pictures, and patterns made up of the bits of our experience. That is why familiarity with the existing material is a prerequisite for new discovery. Even more are we limited in both understanding and expression by our usable vocabularies. We do not get clear ideas from voices using words we do not know. Glossolalia (speaking in tongues) may make us feel good; but it *teaches* us nothing.

Even with words we know, there is the danger of our own special associations. The possibility of "coloring" (well set forth in Chapter 9 of Darby and Joan's psychic classic *Our Unseen Guest*) is always a danger, and we must ever be on the alert to guard against it.

Meditation as a process does not differ in essence from the scientific method. The element essential to both is that the revelation or scientific hypothesis, however arrived at, be *rigorously tested* before it is accepted and adopted as probable truth. No matter how ecstatic the original reception seemed, unless the content stands up under and is confirmed by subsequent experiment (experience), it should not be considered gospel. God gives us minds to reject nonsense and to make sense of our world and our relationships with Him and each other. Neither miasma nor charisma is to be taken on faith; faith is irrelevant where you can *know* (as Paul taught).

Everything should be tested by the mind as to whether it is reasonable and as to whether it works by honest observation. Paul is very specific: "Do not restrain the Holy Spirit; do not despise inspired messages. *Put all things to the test:* keep what is good, and avoid *every kind* of evil" (I Thess. 5:19–22). And Jesus said: Watch out for false prophets; you will know them by the way they act—by their *fruits,* not by what they *say* (Matt. 7:15–20).

After the validity of the result has been established by testing (to the maximum extent by independent verification), then the mind should be used to order and express the new insights gained. The more the mind knows, the more applications and ramifications of the new insights can be suggested and demonstrated. This is the process of real progress in both the spiritual and the scientific areas.

What Is Transcendental Meditation?

Harold H. Bloomfield, Michael Cain, Dennis T. Jaffe, and Al Rubottom

HAROLD H. BLOOMFIELD, M.D., *completed a psychiatric residency at Yale University's School of Medicine. He has written about and conducted workshops on behavior therapy and group therapy. He plans to become a teacher of Transcendental Meditation and to do further research into the applications of TM to medicine and psychiatry.*

MICHAEL CAIN *is an environmental artist and painter who has been teaching Transcendental Meditation since 1970. A research associate at Yale from 1969–73, he has taught a course there on the Science of Creative Intelligence, which explored the relationship of TM to creative intelligence.*

DENNIS T. JAFFE *is a counselor and social researcher with an interest in forms of personal and social change. He is coauthor of* Toward a Radical Therapy *and a forthcoming book on drug use and the youth culture.*

AL RUBOTTOM *has been a teacher of Transcendental Meditation since 1970. He has written about TM for the popular press and professional journals.*

TRANSCENDENTAL MEDITATION (TM) was introduced into the United States by Maharishi (meaning "great seer") Mahesh Yogi, who founded the International Meditation Society, the Students' International Meditation Society, and the Spiritual Regeneration Movement. Since his first visit here in 1959, his technique has gained over 200,000 adherents. Its rapid spread can be traced to its ease and immediate effects: it can be learned in a few hours and is practiced for two fifteen- or twenty-minute periods a day. Reportedly, beneficial mental and physical effects are experienced after the first meditations. Hardly a month goes by without a magazine article documenting profound changes in businessmen, students, drug users, teachers, families, and psychotherapists, who report increased well-being, relaxation, and energy, lessened anxiety, greater perceptiveness, deeper relationships, and the alleviation of mental and physical symptoms of all kinds. They attribute these changes to Transcendental Meditation. Such reports have led to the scientific study of this technique, and the research reports have been so provocative that they have led many scientifically skeptical people to try it themselves. TM is a form of meditation that is particularly suited to active people who want to benefit from a practice without adopting a new religious doctrine or spending weeks or years at a monastic retreat.

TM is not a religion, a philosophy, or a way of life. It is a simple and effortless technique for expanding

"What Is Transcendental Meditation?" was written especially for this volume and is printed by permission of the authors. It is based on their forthcoming book on the psychology of Transcendental Meditation called *Meditation and Stress* (New York: Delacorte, 1974).

conscious awareness, which leads to improvements in many aspects of life. The term "transcendental" means "going beyond," and Maharishi claims that TM offers access to an unlimited reservoir of energy and "creative intelligence" that lies at the source of thought within the deepest layers of the psyche. Contacting this innermost source enables you to realize your unique human potential. This is done by letting your attention flow inward according to its own inclination, not by trying to force or direct it in any way. The experience of pure self-awareness has a profoundly revitalizing effect on all subsequent activity. TM, unlike other meditative practices surrounded by esoteric trappings and philosophies, requires no preparatory rituals, special setting, or unusual posture. It is not a special skill but simply the activation of a potentiality that every human nervous system is structured to enjoy. It can therefore be easily learned and practiced by anyone.

The practice of TM often leads to the experience of pure consciousness, a state of awareness in which you are perfectly alert while deeply relaxed, but not distracted by any specific sense impression, feeling, or thought. Meditators report this experience as "blank awareness," "being awake inside with nothing going on," or "not being asleep, but not being aware of anything in particular." Instead of the ordinary waking state of consciousness, in which you are constantly bombarded by a cascade of impressions, thoughts, and feelings, TM facilitates the experience of a state of restful alertness and pure awareness. This state is not a bizarre or unusual occurrence, for after their first meditation people often remark, "I've been there before" or "I felt that kind of peaceful relaxation when I was a child."

Maharishi suggests that pure awareness is familiar because it is the most fundamental aspect of the self, the source of knowledge and energy that has been described by exceptional people in all cultures throughout history. This fundamental experience of transcendence has been given many names, which together attest to its universality and supreme importance—*samadhi, satori,* Nirvana, the kingdom of heaven within, the Oversoul, the One, the Good, Being, superconsciousness, cosmic consciousness, peak experience, oceanic experience. Recently, Western psychologists such as Carl Jung and Abraham Maslow have begun to look more closely at the powerful curative effects of these experiences and to bring them within the realm of scientific study. TM allows a person to follow a systematic path toward this experience twice a day, making the possibility of self-discovery widely available.

TM consists of thinking a thought called a mantra (a Sanskrit word meaning "sound whose effects are known") over and over again without any effort to exclude other thoughts that intrude. When you learn the technique, a trained instructor selects a specific mantra according to an exact procedure. All mantras have a soothing and restful influence when repeated mentally. Their known effects are thus not due to their meaning, since they have none, but probably to their vibratory quality on the brain.

The sound of the mantra facilitates the inward flow of attention in a process often called mental diving. If during meditation the mantra leaves your awareness, you simply reintroduce it without making any effort to concentrate on it. TM is thus neither a strenuous process of concentration nor a deliberate effort to clear your mind. A meditator soon finds that the process of effortlessly thinking the mantra is not the contradiction it may appear to be. Since the ability to contact pure awareness is not a learned skill, but a naturally uncovered capacity innate in everyone, like speech or walking, it is not really an effort to allow the mind to move toward deeper levels. It is a spontaneously catalytic process which, once begun, becomes progressively deeper and more absorbing. Repeating the mantra allows attention to loosen its attachment to surface-level sense impressions and thoughts. Meditators often experience a state of contentment and relaxation in pure awareness—usually only for a few moments at first, but with greater duration and clarity as practice proceeds.

Meditators characteristically find the inward flow of their attention frequently being interrupted by the intrusion of thoughts, emotions, and sensations, a few of which may even be bizarre or dreamlike. Maharishi emphasizes that this process of stress release does not reflect unsuccessful meditation or something to be avoided. It is rather a recurring by-product of the meditative state—the release of stress from the nervous system. It has been suggested that the released thoughts and emotions constitute an analogue to dreams, which interrupt the nightly cycle of sleep but are necessary for the relief of psychic stress accumulated during the day. After a difficult day, you may experience considerable "unstressing" during meditation: deep and pleasurable periods of pure awareness, followed by the recurrent release of stress that has accumulated in the nervous system. There is no need to analyze or remember the content of thought that occurs in meditation. You simply return to the mantra when you notice you are not thinking it, without trying to push the thought out of your mind.

Many of the beneficial effects of TM on everyday

life are derived from its ability to release accumulations of deep-rooted stress. The potential significance of a natural method of alleviating stress is underscored by the fact that a majority of Americans suffer from hypertension and other stress-related diseases ranging from heart disease and ulcers to anxiety neurosis, headaches, and other psychosomatic ailments. Maharishi defines stress as the physical imprinting in the nervous system of unduly excessive experiences that overload a person's faculties. TM counteracts stress by providing an equal and opposite state of deep rest. Maharishi accounts for this by what Elmer Green of the Menninger Clinic in Topeka calls the psychophysiological principle: For every event or change in consciousness there is a corresponding event or change in physiological functioning.

Every state of consciousness can be correlated with a characteristic physiological state. Just as bodily metabolism is affected by an anxious or angry state of mind, so the opposite is true—that relaxation beneficially affects the mental state. The physiological changes that occur in meditation can be measured to provide data on TM's effects, as we will report later. As a meditator experiences the mantra on subtler levels of thought, his metabolism changes in a measurable way—reduced mental activity allows reduced physical activity. Just as sleep and dreaming allow a complex psychophysiological regeneration to occur, so does TM activate a natural process for dissolving stress. We can conceive of stresses of all kinds as abnormalities that the nervous system tends to reject automatically, in keeping with the organism's innate urge toward health. All weakness is essentially due to lack of strength, and therefore cure or improvement depends upon directly strengthening the individual rather than just studying or coming to grips with the source of the problem. Knowledge of the source of stress may even be so unnecessary as to be demoralizing rather than therapeutic. A review of the current psychological techniques for relieving stress—including psychoanalysis, psychotherapy, group therapy, chemotherapy, and behavior modification—shows that they are either limited to a very few patients; take long years of personal attention from the therapist and lack reliable effectiveness; are specific to only a few kinds of stresses; may tend to restimulate stresses or stressful behavior without replacing them with strength; or merely make the patient manageable, without curing him. Empirical measurements comparing wakeful relaxation, sleep, and TM support the claim that the rest gained through meditation is the deepest possible, and therefore accounts for its powerful regenerative qualities.

By citing both modern Western scientific research and the ancient Vedic spiritual tradition of India, Maharishi explains why the technique of TM provides contact with the deepest center of the self and with what he calls creative intelligence, resulting in greater satisfaction, knowledge, and renewed ability to act creatively and in harmony with nature. The philosophical basis of his teachings are given at length in *The Science of Being and the Art of Living* (published by SRM Books and by Mentor as *Transcendental Meditation*) and in his new translation and commentary *On the Bhagavad Gita* (Penguin). It is too complex to be summarized here, but its essence is derived from the Vedas, which establish the source of all knowledge, not in external objects, but in the inner core of the individual, within pure consciousness. Modern Western culture has developed methods of technological control over the environment, at great sacrifice of knowledge about the self and the attainment of subjective values and truth. Only recently have Western psychologists, philosophers, and social visionaries begun to look for ways to redress the imbalance. They have begun to look at inner experience, at the internal basis of the self, at natural values and biological rhythms and laws, in an attempt to regain a proper balance of subjective and objective knowledge.

Maharishi's achievement has been to adapt the ancient technique and tradition to a modern Western format and to current scientific techniques of verification and communication. His personal background unites the ancient East with the modern West. He was educated at Allahabad University, graduating in 1942 with a degree in physics. Instead of pursuing a technical or business career, however, he became a disciple of his teacher Guru Dev, who transmitted to him both the technique and the philosophy.

Guru Dev taught those who came to him for guidance a technique that originated in the Vedas, the oldest of Hindu (and possibly all human) oral teachings. The technique had been handed down from teacher to teacher within monasteries and in remote places. There had also been several periods when this teaching was made widely available to the public, such as the times of Buddha, Shankara, and Krishna. Guru Dev also made the technique available to all who came, not only to recluses but to those who were leading active lives and had families.

After Guru Dev's passing in 1953, Maharishi himself undertook a reclusive way of life, settling in a Himalayan cave from which he had no intention of emerging. However, as his meditation progressed, he felt some unfavorable influences and decided that his fulfilled consciousness must be responding to some quality in the atmosphere reflecting the sufferings of humanity. He left his retreat to attempt to relieve suffering by offering the technique to all who would receive it.

For months Maharishi traveled alone through India. Because of his monk's costume and appealing appearance, he was often asked to address a small gathering. When he did, he spoke about humanity realizing its full potential through a natural and effortless technique that allowed attention to be drawn within, not by religious conviction, but through a potentiality within everyone's nervous system. His message was enthusiastically received and thousands learned TM.

After about a year of traveling, he was given a ticket to fly to the West. Upon arriving in Hawaii in 1959, without a suitcase or any connections, he met people who set up a public forum for him. After instructing numerous people, he flew to California, where again helpful people set up a lecture program. These first sessions were so well received that a plan was worked out to teach the technique not just to people personally instructed by Maharishi, but in every community throughout the world. Maharishi would "multiply himself" by training teachers and creating a global organization to structure these activities.

Various nonprofit educational organizations were formed, particularly the Students' International Meditation Society (SIMS), as part of the effort to spread effectively the practice of TM. Many people contributed time and money to these efforts, and the first teacher training course was held in Rishikesh, India, in 1961. A second course was held in 1965, and since then courses have been held three times a year in different places for increasingly larger groups. Now more than four thousand TM teachers around the world in various local centers offer introductory and advanced courses of instruction in the practice and its implications. The teaching program has recently been expanded to include a worldwide extension university, Maharishi International University (MIU), which offers videotaped courses, sponsors research on TM, and promotes symposia and academic inquiry into the Science of Creative Intelligence (SCI).

The spread of TM has been facilitated by modern technology. In addition to residential teacher training courses, Maharishi has made a color videotape cassette course in the Science of Creative Intelligence. The "World Plan" goal is to establish a meditation center for every million people in the world, including teacher training facilities. There are currently over two hundred centers in the United States. Formal academic courses on the Science of Creative Intelligence have been taught at over fifty universities, including Yale, Stanford, and UCLA. Maharishi International University has been formed in order to offer more integrated academic programs. The use of videotape hookups at TM centers will make MIU courses available to people all over the world.

Maharishi now acts as a teacher of teachers, and advises the organizations that teach the technique and disseminate information about the results and benefits of regular practice. The introductory courses have been structured to insure precise accuracy of teaching by means of systematic procedures for both teaching the technique and then verifying the correctness of an individual's practice. After learning TM, a person can come at any time for "checking": he meditates with a trained checker who can verify the correctness of his meditation and answer specific questions. There are also weekend residence courses where meditators practice the more intensive process of repeated meditations under careful supervision. This practice, called rounding, intensifies the process of contacting pure awareness and infusing creative intelligence. Meditators return from a weekend residence course feeling refreshed and energized. After about two years of regular practice, meditators are eligible for an advanced course of additional instruction and also may take training courses to become a checker or teacher.

The introductory course takes only a few hours on four consecutive days. All meditation centers offer two free introductory lectures describing the technique and its potentialities. Special lectures are also offered by request for an organization or professional meeting or even for a group of friends at someone's home. If you wish to learn TM after hearing the second lecture, you are interviewed by an instructor and agree to pay the fee ($75 for adults, $45 for college students, $35 for high school students), which covers not only personal instruction, but also four required follow-up sessions, regular checking, optional weekly meetings, and newsletters announcing special events and residence courses.

You then come by appointment for personal instruction. You are asked to bring a few flowers, a white handkerchief, and some fruit, to be used in a brief traditional ceremony performed in Sanskrit, in which the instructor expresses gratitude to the past teachers in the tradition. It is not a religious ceremony because you only witness it. It guarantees that you receive the technique as it has been passed down for centuries. Then you receive a personal mantra, selected by the teacher, and are guided into your first meditation with the teacher. The meditation is practiced at home twice the next day. All the students return the next evening for the first of three group sessions at which your experiences and reactions of the first day are discussed. At these sessions the whole process is more fully explained, so that you can relate what you hear to your own personal experience. After this initial course, meditators are invited to make appointments for personal checking as often as desired. A weekly check is recommended for the first month, and monthly checking thereafter.

While the effects of meditative states of consciousness have been valued since the dawn of humanity, it is only in the past decade that the scientific study of these states has yielded much data. Objective study of consciousness was made possible by the invention of such devices as the electroencephalograph, which measures the electrical activity of the brain through the intact skull, and computers, which unscramble the various brain waves into coherent patterns. Other physiological functions are correlated with different states of consciousness. Muscle tension, heart rate, blood pressure, rate of respiration, and the electrical resistance of the skin are measurable, and provide valuable insight into the connection between physiology and a person's subjective states of conscious awareness.

Nathaniel Kleitman and his associates in a sleep laboratory at the University of Chicago undertook the first studies that differentiated physiological correlates of the three common states of consciousness—sleeping, dreaming, and wakefulness. Studies of Zen monks, Indian yogis, and, recently, Transcendental Meditators in the United States have begun to provide evidence that suggests that meditative states of consciousness are quite different from the three ordinary states and have quite different physiological correlates and effects.

In addition to finding objective measures of various internal states, investigators of meditative states of consciousness have had difficulty in finding suitable subjects who were adept at their technique and in getting them to practice their meditations with monitoring devices like a mask over the mouth and nose to measure oxygen consumption, catheters in an artery in the arm to measure changes in blood chemistry, and electrodes connected to the skull and skin.

The recent spread of TM made it possible for large numbers of subjects to be studied in well-controlled laboratory settings. Because the practitioners were normal people, not religious ascetics, the results could not be attributed to factors like diet or the religious community. Also, the ease of TM meant that it could be practiced without disruption under laboratory conditions. For these reasons Dr. Robert Keith Wallace and Dr. Herbert Benson, of Harvard Medical School, chose TM for the most comprehensive study of the physiological correlates of a meditative technique. Thirty-six subjects of both sexes, some in Boston and some in Los Angeles, ages seventeen to forty-one and without physical or mental disabilities, participated in the initial study. They had practiced TM from one week to nine years, averaging two and a half years.

The procedure was simple. After half an hour for relaxing and getting used to the instruments, each subject sat quietly for about twenty minutes. This provided base-line measurements for each person, with which the changes during and after meditation could be compared. The subject was then instructed to meditate for the normal period of time, usually twenty minutes, and then to remain quietly seated for another half hour, to obtain a comparative set of post-meditation measurements. The three series of measurements were then compared.

Wallace and Benson's findings, reported in numerous articles, including the February 1972 issue of *Scientific American*, added considerably to the sketchy, often contradictory and erratic information from previous studies of yogis and Zen meditators. One of the most dramatic changes they recorded was a decrease in oxygen consumption. This is generally regarded as a measure of the level of physical activity, since it increases during exertion and decreases during rest. During deep sleep it drops to a point about 10 per cent below normal. Wallace and Benson found in all meditators an immediate, spontaneous reduction in oxygen consumption of 16–18 per cent. This began during the first minutes of meditation and was consistently sustained throughout. After meditation, oxygen consumption returned to normal, premeditation levels, indicating a return to a metabolic level ready for activity. To insure that their findings were not due to suggestibility or the mood of subjects in that setting, the changes were compared to changes reported for subjects under hypnosis. No decrease in oxygen consumption was found under hypnosis. Wallace confirmed that the decrease in oxygen was a natural phenomenon by checking that the decrease was accompanied by a decrease in carbon dioxide metabolism— another indication that the physical system is relaxed and functioning naturally, though at a slower rate, and not under any strain due to the decrease.

They also found a large increase in the galvanic skin response (GSR), which is the resistance of the surface of the skin to an electric current. This is widely used as a measure of decreased anxiety and is the basis of many tests, the most famous being the lie detector.

If a person is relaxed and calm, not tense, the GSR increases. During deep sleep it increases by about 200 per cent. During TM, GSR increased by as much as 500 per cent in some subjects, indicating even greater relaxation and lessened anxiety. Dr. David Orme-Johnson reports in a 1973 issue of the *Journal of Psychosomatic Medicine* that Transcendental Meditators recover more quickly from stressful stimuli and have greater physiological stability than a similar group of nonmeditating students. Meditators recovered quickly when subjected to a sudden stimulus (a very loud noise), their GSR decreasing sharply for a few seconds and then quickly returning to normal. This autonomic stability has been correlated with measures of mental health. This state of calm alertness has measurable perceptual effects as well. Robert Shaw and David Kolb, of the University of Texas, found that TM practitioners had a faster reaction time than nonmeditators, and Graham, at the University of Sussex, England, found increased auditory acuity.

Another change reported by Wallace and Benson that strongly suggests decreased anxiety is the decrease in subjects' blood lactate, which was reduced by about 33 per cent compared to the drop in that of someone lying down or in the subjects' own premeditation relaxed state. The drop also occurred at a much faster rate (300 per cent faster) than it does during sleep. F. N. Pitts reported in a 1969 article in *Scientific American* that people suffering from anxiety neurosis increase their blood lactate when subjected to stress, and even more strikingly, they become anxious when given injections of lactate. Furthermore, patients with high blood pressure often show elevated blood lactate levels in a resting state. The low lactate level found in the TM subjects thus appears to correlate with their reported decreased anxiety and deep relaxation.

This biochemical change among meditators suggests a possible mechanism that accounts for their increased sense of well-being and decreased anxiety, and suggests that TM may be helpful for people suffering from hypertension. These findings led Wallace and Benson to conclude that the relaxation of TM was in some way a physiological counterpart to the "fight or flight" defense alarm reaction, which mobilizes the body to respond to threats and imminent danger or stress. Many people have suggested that our culture—with its tremendous psychological pressures, constant sensory overstimulation, and minimal physical activity—keeps us in an almost constant state of inner alarm, leading to stress and its related ailments. TM appears to slow down or counteract this alarm reaction and its physically and psychically destructive effects.

Another aspect of the Wallace-Benson research involved monitoring their subjects' brain waves. The characteristic change was an increase in slow alpha waves in the frontal and central regions of the brain, accompanied in some subjects by rhythmical theta trains, which are even slower waves, in the front of the brain. The frequencies and patterns are quite different from those seen in sleep and dreaming.

The TM brain wave pattern is consistent with Kasamatsu and Hirai's findings with Zen monks who had been meditating for ten to twenty years and is thus a remarkable demonstration of the speed with which the TM technique produces similar results.[1] As in the Zen study, Wallace found that incoming stimuli were

[1] However, similarity in physiological processes does not automatically grant spiritual growth and psychological maturity. *Editor.*

experienced by the brain clearly and freshly, but at the same time without interrupting the state of relaxation.

The meditative state is characterized by both heightened awareness and relaxation, so that one is not disturbed by every stimulus. Relaxation is associated with increased alpha waves. Studies of alpha conditioning, by which a subject learns to increase his alpha wave production, found that the alpha state corresponds with reports of pleasant, restful, tranquil emotional states. Research in progress at the Institute of Living, a private psychiatric hospital in Hartford, Connecticut, has looked in precise detail at the changes in brain waves in patients who have been taught either TM or alpha conditioning as an adjunct to psychotherapy. Preliminary findings suggest that TM is more relaxing and pleasurable for patients and may lead to more profound therapeutic results than alpha training. It also confirms and adds to the picture of brain waves during TM.

These and other studies demonstrate that TM has profound effects on the body. It sets in motion an integrated complex of physiological changes in the direction of relaxation, decreased anxiety, and a greater sense of well-being. These changes have led researchers to begin to define a physiologic state that is so different from the normal states—sleeping, dreaming, and waking—that Wallace has suggested it qualifies as a fourth major state of consciousness. He surveyed 394 regular meditators regarding their health; 84 per cent reported significant improvement in mental health, with most citing specific, concrete indications such as increased grades, lessened fears, and better personal relationships, and 67 per cent reported significant improvement in physical health, such as fewer colds, headaches, allergies, or even cessation of chronic ailments.

The effects on mental health suggest that TM can be conceived as a kind of self-administered psychotherapy. Therapy is available to relatively few people, is very costly, and does not produce consistent results for all patients. Therefore, meditation may be a very important additional tool for relieving psychological suffering. Daniel Goleman (see "Meditation as Metatherapy," p. 181 of this volume) argues that meditation is a metatherapy that systematically decreases anxieties; he stresses the use of mechanisms that are familiar to therapists but that are more consistently and better applied through meditation. Meditation is suggested by more and more therapists, including two of the authors, to their patients. Preliminary reports suggest that meditation greatly enhances and speeds up the process of therapy, leads to deeper access into the psyche, and produces consistently better results than therapy without meditation. Its deep relaxation certainly contributes to its efficacy, but in addition we suggest that additional psychological effects of the experience of pure awareness favorably affect the patient's ability to deal with disturbing or unpleasant psychic material with a minimum of anxiety.

The most extensive research project using Transcendental Meditation as an adjunct to psychotherapy is being conducted at the Institute of Living and is headed by the director of research, Dr. Bernard C. Glueck. After nine months (as of this writing, June 1973) about sixty patients have learned TM; other groups have been taught alpha biofeedback conditioning and relaxation techniques to provide comparative data. Careful records are kept of their physiological changes; their progress in therapy; their behavior in the hospital community; their feelings about the treatment; their performance in school, if they are students (the institute has an accredited high school program); and what happens after they leave the hospital. Several teachers of TM are on the project staff, and members of the clinical staff have learned to meditate. From data gathered thus far, Dr. Glueck reports significant rates of improvement in the patients who practice TM, generally faster than previously. In addition, TM is well received by the patients, who feel that they are in control of the process and are responsible for the benefits they gain from the practice. This is in contrast to the psychoactive drugs, which, although recognized by the patient as helpful, do not give the same sense of "helping myself." Many have been able to reduce their need for medication, with marked improvement of sleep disorders.

The process of meditation apparently leads to an intimate and cumulative contact with the core of the self. This in turn promotes the process of self-discovery and growth. The resources of consciousness provided by the experience of pure awareness—the proposed fourth state of consciousness characterized by deep rest and mental alertness—seem to catalyze growth through the neurophysiological integration of the nervous system. Charles Tart, who has studied altered states of consciousness for several years and practiced TM for two years, reported in a 1971 article in the *Journal of Transpersonal Psychology* that the unstressing process seems to be a "psychic lubricant" that allows the release and settling of inappropriately processed experiences. In this sense TM may serve as a sort of "self-analysis" which proceeds naturally without any conscious direction or attempt to master one's past or present personality. Dr. Glueck notes that the thought content one may notice in meditation, though often of a primitive or even charged nature, is seldom if ever accompanied by the usual emotional charge or effect one feels in similar recollections drawn out during psychoanalysis or psychotherapy. He finds that some meditating patients can "work through" the significance of this material in relation to their illness in a much shorter period of time than is ordinarily the case—presumably because they are less bothered by recalling it in analysis or therapy after already having had it "played out" during meditation.

Many recent studies focus on the greater psychological health of persons who practice TM. Sanford Nidich, William Seeman, and Thomas Banta in the May 1972 issue of *Journal of Counselling Psychology* compared the responses of fifteen undergraduate meditators with a control group. They used a well-known measure of self-actualization, the Personality Orientation Inventory, which measures characteristics of healthy, loving, creative, fully functioning people suggested by the work and writings of the late Abraham Maslow. They found that a meditator's sense of inner-directedness increases, as do the ability to express feelings in spontaneous action, the acceptance of aggression, and the capacity for intimate contact. Meditators seem to have better "psychic gyroscopes" and are more open to their own and to others' deep experiences and feelings.

Maynard Shelly, of the University of Kansas, reports on many years of studying the production and measurement of happiness in his book *Sources of Satisfaction*. His theory postulates that each individual has an optimum physiological level of arousal, below which lies boredom or unpleasantness. Some people prefer quiet, sustained pleasures, like reading or sitting with a loved one, whereas others enjoy highly exciting, risky, or stimulating pleasures, like mountain climbing. Every person has a unique ratio of both kinds of pleasure that makes him happy, and Shelly's work measures the degree to which a person reaches that optimum state. Shelly's students Landrith and Davies conducted several studies measuring the changes in happiness reported by samples of over one hundred Transcendental Meditators; the changes in these measures as their practice continued; and the responses of a control group of similar students who did not meditate. While people who started TM scored slightly lower than the control group in happiness, after a few months to a year of TM they seem happier and more relaxed; they experience a feeling of enjoyment more often; they seek arousal as much as nonmeditators (but avoid extreme excitements); they seek social contacts as often as nonmeditators despite the fact that they tend to spend more time alone; they develop deeper interpersonal relationships; and they depend less on their external environment to provide them with happiness, while relying more on themselves. Greater happiness, stability, self-sufficiency, and deeper contact with others seem to characterize meditators, and these measures increase as they meditate longer. Shelly suggests that meditators have more personal resources and energy to mobilize for their goals and are less affected by environmental setbacks. The results of all these studies suggest that TM is a unique psychophysiological process through which personal awareness of self, others, and the environment increases, along with the ability to achieve one's goals.

A great deal of the publicity about TM has come from studies, by Benson and Wallace among others, that report meditators decreasing drug use—not only illegal drugs but prescription drugs, alcohol, and cigarettes. Several studies, one involving almost two thousand meditators reported by Barbara Marzetta, Herbert Benson, and R. Keith Wallace in the September 1972 issue of *Medical Counterpoint*, show that over time, meditators lose interest in whatever drugs they had been taking. Of course, many young people turn from drugs to TM when they realize that the benefits they seek from drugs are not permanent, and they are therefore predisposed to cut down or stop drug use. Still, the response of adult drug users, who smoke, drink, and take tranquilizers or sleeping pills, tend in the same direction. Reports from therapists indicate that use of prescription drugs decreases as patients find TM lessening their anxiety and enabling them to sleep more easily. Similar evidence confirmed by newer studies has led drug abuse programs to investigate and offer TM as a way of helping drug-dependent people.

Several institutions—schools, prisons, and a business —have co-operated with researchers in conducting related studies that include the use of TM. These projects do not attempt to evaluate TM as a cure for illness but rather as a general method of helping people to improve their functioning and to enhance their well-being. In many instances, after an administrator or executive begins TM, he encourages others to try it and often asks a TM teacher to speak to his colleagues or employees. Numerous anecdotal accounts describe how one or more persons have introduced TM into an office, organization, or business, with positive effects for all who begin the practice.

Stephen B. Cox reported in the *Kentucky Law Review* on a study conducted at the La Tuna Federal Penitentiary in Texas. Twenty-three volunteer inmates/addicts were instructed in TM. Although results are not yet published in final form, preliminary reports are promising. David Ballou has reported informally on a project in the Stillwater State Prison in Minnesota, where fifty inmates were offered TM. Those who began TM were checked regularly and evaluated by a variety of measures. The results were positive in all the areas noted by other studies—decreased anxiety, reduced drug use, increased sense of well-being, and more positive motivation. Edward Morler is presently at work on a doctoral study of TM's effects in an organizational context. He is testing how the use of TM by employees in a bank will affect individual job performance. Several unofficial reports from public and private secondary schools suggest that meditating students improve their work, interact more easily with other students, their parents, and faculty, and voluntarily reduce their use of drugs. These accounts suggest that the personal benefits of TM carry over into a meditator's environment. One can only speculate about what might occur if school systems or corporations were to introduce TM. (In 1972 Haile Selassie, Emperor of Ethiopia, approved and began the introduction of TM into the entire public school system of Ethiopia.)

Evidence from psychotherapy, clinical neurology, child psychology, and studies of creativity support the basic tenet that the direction of human life is not arbitrary but is evolving along a definite path toward the actualization of maximum potential. The basic urge or drive in life is toward the full expression of one's talents and innate potentiality. The growing body of research evidence, supported by meditators' testimony, suggests that TM liberates previously untapped resources for the realization of these human potentialities. The truly miraculous capacities of the human brain and nervous system are still only partially understood at best and hence far from fully appreciated. Medical researchers are finding that fundamentally vital resources for improvements in health and wellbeing are found within the individual. Clearly the hope of our physical and psychical healers lies in effectively tapping these vital resources to achieve neurophysiological integration and the subsequent achievement of fuller mental potential.

This unlimited mental potential can be experienced as pure consciousness. When contacted regularly through the daily practice of TM, the value of this purely subjective awareness is infused into the mind and removes the limitations on the mind's full range of capabilities. The key to successful psychotherapy or to the most complete development of the normal individual is to create those physiological conditions that optimize the natural tendency of the nervous system to rejuvenate and reintegrate itself. TM can be learned easily and practiced naturally. It produces beneficial effects spontaneously exactly because it operates on the basis of this innate tendency. The ease and simplicity of the technique often seem startling to those who expect improved physical or mental health to be found through modern medical inventions or therapies, just because pathology and the allopathic alleviation of symptoms have been dwelt upon excessively in our society.

We can see that the optimal condition TM provides is simply a mode of functioning native to the human organism, maximizing deep rest and mental alertness. As the study of this proposed fourth state of consciousness proceeds, we expect to learn much more about the experience of pure awareness, its physiological correlates, and its effects. So far the consensus is favorable. As this knowledge spreads, the introduction of TM in schools, businesses, and communities will help to reduce the anxiety from which so many people suffer needlessly and to increase their growth and "self-actualization." Maharishi has said that man is born to enjoy and that suffering is alien to life. We find nearly all the prominent psychologists of the past several decades agree in their conclusion that man has an unchanging, intrinsically good inner nature that supports the growth of a healthy, happy, and fruitful life. The practice of TM will undoubtedly serve to make this inner strength available to more and more members of our society.

Meditation in Action

Chogyam Trungpa

CHOGYAM TRUNGPA *is a Tibetan Buddhist who makes his residence in the United States at Tail of the Tiger Meditation Center in Barnet, Vermont, and at Karma Dzong in Boulder, Colorado. His autobiography is entitled* Born in Tibet.

MEDITATION IS A VAST SUBJECT, and there have been many developments throughout the ages and many variations among the different religious traditions. But broadly speaking the basic character of meditation takes on one of two forms. The first stems from the teachings that are concerned with the discovery of the nature of existence; the second concerns communication with the external or universal concept of God. In either case meditation is the only way to put the teachings into practice.

Where there is the concept of an external, "higher" being, there is also an internal personality—which is known as "I" or the ego. In this case meditation practice becomes a way of developing communication with an external being. This means that one feels oneself to be inferior and one is trying to contact something higher, greater. Such meditation is based on devotion. This is basically an inward, or introvert, practice of meditation, which is well known in the Hindu teachings, where the emphasis is on going into the inward state of *samadhi,* into the depths of the heart. One finds a similar technique practiced in the orthodox teachings of Christianity, where the prayer of the heart is used and concentration on the heart is emphasized. This is a means of identifying oneself with an external being and necessitates purifying oneself. The basic belief is that one is separate from God, but there is still a link, one is still part of God. This confusion sometimes arises, and in order to clarify it one has to work inward and try to raise the standard of individuality to the level of a higher consciousness. This approach makes use of emotions and devotional practices that are aimed at making contact with God or gods or some particular saint. These devotional practices may also include the recitation of mantra.

The other principal form of meditation is almost entirely opposite in its approach, though finally it might lead to the same results. Here there is no belief in higher and lower; the idea of different levels, or of being in an underdeveloped state, does not arise. One does not feel inferior, and what one is trying to achieve is not something higher than oneself. Therefore, the practice of meditation does not require an inward concentration on the heart. There is no centralizing concept at all. Even such practices as concentrating on the *chakras,* or psychic centers of the body, are approached in a different way. Although in certain teachings of Buddhism the concept of chakras is mentioned, the practices connected with them are not based on the development of an inward center. So this basic form of meditation is concerned with trying to see what *is*. There are many variations on this form of meditation, but they are generally based on various techniques for opening oneself. The achievement of this kind of meditation is not, therefore, the result of some long-term, arduous practice through which we build ourselves up into a "higher" state, nor does it necessitate going into any kind of inner trance state. It is rather what one might call "working meditation" or extrovert meditation, where skillful means and wisdom must be combined like the two wings of a bird. This is not a question of trying to retreat from the world. In fact without the external world, the world of apparent phenomena, meditation would be almost impossible to practice, for the individual and the external world are not separate, but merely coexist. Therefore, the concept of trying to communicate and trying to become one with some higher being does not arise.

In this kind of meditation practice of the concept of *nowness* plays a very important part. In fact, it is the essence of meditation. Whatever one does, whatever one tries to practice, is not aimed at achieving a higher state or at following some theory or ideal, but simply, without any object or ambition, trying to see what is here and now. One has to become aware of the present moment through such means as concentrating on the breathing, a practice that has been developed in the Buddhist tradition. This is based on developing the knowledge of nowness, for each respiration is unique, it is an expression of *now*. Each breath is separate from the next and is fully seen and fully felt, not in a visualized form, nor simply as an aid to concentration, but it should be fully and properly dealt with. Just as a very hungry man, when he is eating, is not even conscious that he is eating food. He is so engrossed in the food that he completely identifies himself with what he is doing and almost becomes one with the taste and enjoyment of it. Similarly with the breathing, the whole idea is to try to see through that very moment in time. So in this case the concept of trying to become something higher does not arise at all, and opinions do not have much importance. In a sense opinions provide a way to escape; they create a kind of slothfulness and obscure one's clarity of vision. The clarity of our consciousness is veiled by prefabricated concepts and whatever we see we try to fit into some pigeonhole or in some way make it fit in with our preconceived ideas. So concepts and theories— and, for that matter, theology—can become obstacles. One might ask, therefore, what is the point of studying Buddhist philosophy? Since there are scriptures and texts and there is surely some philosophy to believe in, wouldn't that also be a concept? Well, that depends on the individual, but basically it is not so. From the start one tries to transcend concepts, and one tries, perhaps in a very critical way, to find out what *is*. One has to develop a critical mind which will stimulate intelligence. This may at first cause one to reject what is said by teachers or what is written in books, but then gradually one begins to feel something and to find something for oneself. That is what is known as the meeting of imagination and reality, where the feeling of certain words and concepts meets with intuitive knowledge, perhaps in a rather vague and imprecise way. One may be uncertain whether what one is learning is right or not, but there is a general feeling that one is about to discover something. One cannot really start by being perfect, but one must start with something. And if one cultivates this intelligent, intuitive insight, then gradually, stage by stage, the real intuitive feeling develops and the imaginary or hallucinatory element is gradually clarified and eventually dies out. Finally that vague feeling of discovery becomes very clear, so that almost no doubt remains. Even at this stage it is possible that one may be unable to explain one's discovery verbally or write it down exactly on paper, and in fact if one tried to do so it would be limiting one's scope and would be rather dangerous. Nevertheless, as this feeling grows and develops one finally attains direct knowledge, rather than achieving something that is separate from oneself. As in the analogy of the hungry man, you become one with the subject. This can only be achieved through the practice of meditation. Therefore, meditation is very much a matter of exercise—it is a working practice. It is not a question of going into some inward depth, but of widening and expanding outward.

These are the basic differences between the two types of meditation practice. The first may be more suitable for some people and the second may be more suitable for others. It is not a question of one being superior or more accurate than the other. But for any form of meditation one must first overcome that great feeling of demand and ambition which acts as a major obstacle. Making demands on a person, such as a guru, or having the ambition to achieve something out of what one is doing, arises out of a built-up desire or wantingness; and that wantingness is a centralized notion. This centralized notion is basically blind. It is like having only one eye, and that one eye being situated in the chest. When you try to walk you cannot turn your head round and you can only see a limited area. Because you can see in only one direction the intelligence of turning the head is lacking. Therefore, there is a great danger of falling. This wantingness acts as a veil and becomes an obstacle to the discovery of the moment of nowness, because the wanting is based either on the future or on trying to continue something that existed in the past, so the nowness is completely forgotten. There may be a certain effort to focus on the nowness, but perhaps only 20 per cent of the consciousness is based on the present and the rest is scattered into the past or the future. Therefore, there is not enough force to see directly what is there.

Here, too, the teaching of selflessness plays a very important part. This is not merely a question of denying the existence of ego, for ego is something relative. Where there is an external person, a higher being, or the concept of something that is separate from oneself, then we tend to think that because there is something outside there must be something here as well. The external phenomenon sometimes becomes such an overwhelming thing and seems to have all sorts of seductive or aggressive qualities, so we erect a kind of defense mechanism against it, failing to see that that is itself a continuity of the external thing. We try to segregate ourselves from the external, and this creates a kind of gigantic bubble in us which consists of nothing but air and water or, in this case, fear and the reflection of the external thing. So this huge bubble prevents any fresh air from coming in, and that is "I" —the ego. So in that sense there is the existence of ego, but it is in fact illusory. Having established that, one generally wants to create some external idol or refuge. Subconsciously one knows that this "I" is only a bubble and it could burst at any moment, so one tries to protect it as much as one can—either consciously or subconsciously. In fact we have achieved such skill at protecting this ego that we have managed to preserve it for hundreds of years. It is as though a person has a very precious pair of spectacles that he puts in a box or various containers in order to keep it safe, so that even if other things are broken this would be preserved. He may feel that other things could bear hardship, but he knows that this could not, so this would last longer. In the same way, ego lasts longer just because one feels it could burst at any time. There is fear of it being destroyed because that would be too much, one would feel too exposed. And there is such character, such a fascinating pattern established outside us, although it is in fact our own reflection. That is why the concept of egolessness is not really a question of whether there is a self or not, or, for that matter, whether there is the existence of God or not; it is rather the taking away of that concept of the bubble. Having done so, one doesn't have to deliberately destroy the ego or deliberately condemn God. And when that barrier is removed one can expand and swim through straight away. But this can only be achieved through the practice of meditation, which must be approached in a very practical and simple way. Then the mystical experience of joy or grace, or whatever it might be, can be found in every object. That is what one tries to achieve through *vipassana*, or "insight" meditation practice. Once we have established a basic pattern of discipline and we have developed a regular way of dealing with the situation—whether it is breathing or walking or what-have-you—then at some stage the technique gradually dies out. Reality gradually expands so that we do not have to use the technique at all. And in this case one does not have to concentrate inward, but one can expand outward more and more. And the more one expands, the closer one gets to the realization of centerless existence.

That is the basic pattern of this kind of meditation, which is based on three fundamental factors: firstly, not centralizing inward; secondly, not having any longing to become higher; and thirdly, becoming completely identified with here and now. These three elements run right through the practice of meditation, from the beginning up to the moment of realization.

Q. You mentioned nowness in your talk, and I was wondering how it is possible to become aware of the absolute through awareness of a relative moment in time?

A. Well, we have to start by working through the relative aspect, until finally this nowness takes on such a living quality that it is no longer dependent on a relative way of expressing nowness. One might say that *now* exists all the time, beyond the concept of relativity. But since all concepts are based on the idea of relativity, it is impossible to find any words that go beyond that. So nowness is the only way to see directly. First it is between the past and the future—now. Then gradually one discovers that nowness is not dependent on relativity at all. One discovers that the past does not exist, the future does not exist, and everything happens now. Similarly, in order to express space one might have first to create a vase, and then one has to break it, and then one sees that the emptiness in the vase is the same as the emptiness outside. That is the whole meaning of technique. At first that nowness is, in a sense, not perfect. Or one might even say that the meditation is not perfect, it is a purely man-made practice. One sits and tries to be still and concentrates on the breathing, and so on. But then, having started in that way, one gradually discovers something more than that. So the effort one has put into it—into the discovery of nowness, for example—would not be wasted, though at the same time one might see that it was rather foolish. But that is the only way to start.

Q. For meditation, would a student have to rid himself of ego before he started, or would this come naturally as he is studying?

A. This comes naturally because you can't start without ego. And basically ego isn't bad. Good and bad doesn't really exist anywhere, it is only a secondary thing. Ego is, in a sense, a false thing, but it isn't necessarily bad. You have to start with ego, and use ego, and from there it gradually wears out, like a pair of shoes. But you have to use it and wear it out thoroughly, so it is not preserved. Otherwise, if you try to push ego aside and start perfect, you may become more and more perfect in a rather one-sided way, but the same amount of imperfection is building up on the other side, just as creating intense light creates intense darkness as well.

Q. You mentioned that there are two basic forms of meditation—devotional practice, or trying to communicate with something higher, and the other one, which is simply awareness of what is—but this devotional practice still plays a part in Buddhism as well, and you have devotional chants and so on, but I am not quite sure how this comes in. I mean, the two appear to be different, so can they in fact be combined?

A. Yes, but the kind of devotional practice that is found in Buddhism is merely a process of opening, of surrendering the ego. It is a process of creating a container. I don't mean to condemn the other kind of devotion, but if one looks at it from the point of view of a person who has an unskillful way of using that

technique, then devotion becomes a longing to free
oneself. One sees oneself as being very separate, and
as being imprisoned and imperfect. One regards oneself as basically bad, and one is trying to break out. In
other words the imperfection part of oneself is identified with "I" and anything perfect is identified with
some external being, so all that is left is trying to get
through the imprisonment. This kind of devotion is
an overemphasized awareness of ego, the negative aspect of ego. Although there are hundreds of variations
of devotional practice in Buddhism, and there are many
accounts of devotion to gurus, or being able to communicate with the guru, and of achieving the Awakened State of mind through devotion. But in these
cases devotion is always begun without centralizing on
the ego. In any chants or ceremonies, for example,
which make use of symbolism, or the visualization of
Buddhas, before any visualization is created there is
first a formless meditation, which creates an entirely
open space. And at the end one always recites what
is known as the Threefold Wheel: "I do not exist;
the external visualization does not exist: and the act
of visualizing does not exist"—the idea being that any
feeling of achievement is thrown back to the openness,
so one doesn't feel that one is collecting anything. I
think that is the basic point. One may feel a great deal
of devotion, but that devotion is a kind of abstract
form of devotion, which does not centralize inwardly.
One simply identifies with that feeling of devotion,
and that's all. This is perhaps a different concept of
devotion, where no center exists, but only devotion
exists. Whereas, in the other case devotion contains
a demand. There is an expectation of getting something out of it in return.

Q. Is there not a great fear generated when we get to this point of opening up and surrendering?

A. Fear is one of the weapons of ego. It protects the ego. If one reaches the stage where one begins to see the folly of ego, then there is fear of losing the ego, and fear is one of its last weapons. Beyond that point fear no longer exists, because the object of fear is to frighten somebody, and when that somebody is not there, then fear loses its function. You see, fear is continually given life by your response, and when there is no one to respond to the fear—which is ego loss—then fear ceases to exist.

Q. You are talking about the ego as an object?

A. In what sense?

Q. In the sense that it is part of the external environment.

A. Ego is, as I have already said, like a bubble. It is an object up to a point, because although it does not really exist—it is an impermanent thing—it in fact shows itself as an object more than actually being one. That is another way of protecting oneself, of trying to maintain ego.

Q. This is an aspect of the ego?

A. Yes.

Q. Then you can't destroy the ego, or you would lose the power to recognize, the power to cognate.

A. No, not necessarily. Because ego does not contain understanding, it does not contain any insight at all. Ego exists in a false way all the time and can only create confusion, whereas insight is something more than that.

Q. Would you say that ego is a secondary phenomenon rather than a primary phenomenon?

A. Yes, very much so. In a sense ego is wisdom, but ego happens to be ignorant as well. You see, when you

realize that you are ignorant, that is the beginning
of the discovery of wisdom—it is wisdom itself.

Q. How does one decide in oneself whether ego is
ignorance or wisdom?

A. It is not really a question of deciding. It is simply that one sees in that way. You see, basically there
is no solid substance, although we talk about ego existing as a solid thing having various aspects. But in fact
it merely lives through time as a continual process
of creation. It is continually dying and being reborn
all the time. Therefore, ego doesn't really exist. But
ego also acts as a kind of wisdom: when ego dies, that
is wisdom itself, and when ego is first formulated, that
is the beginning of ignorance itself. So wisdom and ego
are not really separate at all. It seems rather difficult
to define, and in a way one would be happier if there
was clear-cut black and white, but somehow that is not
the natural pattern of existence. There is no clear-cut
black and white at all, and all things are interdepend-
ent. Darkness is an aspect of light, and light is an aspect
of darkness, so one can't really condemn one side and
build up everything on the other. It is left entirely to
the individual to find his own way, and it is possible
to do so. It is the same for a dog who has never swum
—if he was suddenly thrown in the water he could
swim. Similarly, we have a kind of spiritual instinct in
us and if we are willing to open ourselves then somehow we find our way directly. It is only a question of
opening up and one doesn't have to have a clear-cut
definition at all.

Q. Would you care to sum up the purpose of meditation?

A. Well, meditation is dealing with purpose itself.
It is not that meditation is for something, but it is
dealing with the aim. Generally we have a purpose

for whatever we do: something is going to happen in the future, therefore what I am doing now is important —everything is related to that. But the whole idea of meditation is to develop an entirely different way of dealing with things, where you have no purpose at all. In fact meditation is dealing with the question of whether or not there is such a thing as purpose. And when one learns a different way of dealing with the situation, one no longer has to have a purpose. One is not on the way to somewhere. Or rather, one is on the way and one is also at the destination at the same time. That is really what meditation is for.

Q. Would you say, then, that it would be a merging with reality?

A. Yes, because reality is there all the time. Reality is not a separate entity, so it is a question of becoming one with reality, or of being in reality—not *achieving* oneness, but becoming identified with it. One is already a part of that reality, so all that remains is to take away the doubt. Then one discovers that one has been there all the time.

Q. Would it be correct to describe it as the realization that the visible is not reality?

A. The visible? Can you define a bit more?

Q. I am thinking of William Blake's theory of the merging of the observer with the observed, and the visible not being the reality at all.

A. Visible things in this sense are reality. There is nothing beyond nowness, therefore what we see is reality. But because of our usual way of seeing things, we do not see them exactly as they are.

Q. Would you say, then, that each person is an individual and must find an individual way toward that?

A. Well, I think that brings us back to the question of ego, which we have been talking about. You see,

there is such a thing as personality, in a way, but we
are not really individuals as separate from the environment, or as separate from external phenomena. That
is why a different approach is necessary. Whereas, if
we were individuals and had no connection with the
rest of things, then there would be no need for a different technique which would lead to oneness. The point
is that there is appearance of individuality, but this
individuality is based on relativity. If there is individuality, there must also be oneness as well.

Q. Yes, but it is the individuality that makes for
oneness. If we weren't individuals, we couldn't be one.
Is that so?

A. Well, the word "individual" is rather ambiguous.
At the beginning individuality may be overemphasized,
because there are various individual aspects. Even when
we reach the stage of realization there is perhaps an
element of compassion, an element of wisdom, an element of energy, and all sorts of different variations.
But what we describe as an individual is something
more than that. We tend to see it as one character with
many things built onto it, which is a way of trying
to find some sort of security. When there is wisdom,
we try to load everything onto it, and it then becomes
an entirely separate entity, a separate person—which
is not so. But still there are individual aspects, there
is individual character. So in Hinduism one finds different aspects of God, different deities, and different
symbols. When one attains oneness with reality, that
reality is not just one single thing, but one can see
from a very wide angle.

Q. If a student has a receptive mind and wishes to
make himself at one with nature, can he be taught
how to meditate, or does he have to develop his own
form?

A. Nature? How do you mean?

Q. If he wishes to study, can he accept other people's teaching, or can he develop them himself?

A. In fact it is necessary to receive oral instruction, oral teaching. Though he must learn to give before he can accept anything, he must learn to surrender. Secondly, he finds that the whole idea of learning stimulates his understanding. Also this avoids building up a great feeling of achievement, as though everything is "my own work"—the concept of the self-made man.

Q. Surely that is not sufficient reason for going to receive instruction from a teacher, just to avoid the feeling that otherwise everything is self-made. I mean, in the case of someone like Ramana Maharshi, who attained realization without an external teacher, surely he shouldn't go and find a guru just in case he might become big-headed?

A. No. But he is exceptional, that is the whole point. There is a way, it is possible. And basically no one can transmit or impart anything to anybody. One has to discover within oneself. So perhaps in certain cases people could do that. But building up on oneself is somehow similar to ego's character, isn't it? One is on rather dangerous ground. It could easily become ego's activity, because there is already the concept of "I" and then one wants to build up more on that side. I think—and this may sound simple, but it is really the whole thing—that one learns to surrender gradually, and that surrendering of the ego is a very big subject. Also, the teacher acts as a kind of mirror, the teacher gives back one's own reflection. Then for the first time you are able to see how beautiful you are, or how ugly you are.

Perhaps I should mention here one or two small

points about meditation, although we have already discussed the general background of the subject.

Generally, meditation instruction cannot be given in a class. There has to be a personal relationship between teacher and pupil. Also there are certain variations within each basic technique, such as awareness of breathing. But perhaps I should briefly mention the basic way of meditating, and then, if you want to go further, I am sure you could do so and receive further instruction from a meditation teacher.

As we have mentioned already, this meditation is not concerned with trying to develop concentration. Although many books on Buddhism speak of such practices as *samatha* as being the development of concentration, I think this term is misleading in a way. One might get the idea that the practice of meditation could be put to commercial use, and that one would be able to concentrate on counting money or something like that. But meditation is not just for commercial uses, it is a different concept of concentration. You see, generally one cannot really concentrate. If one tries very hard to concentrate, then one needs the thought that is concentrating on the subject and also something that makes that accelerate further. Thus there are two processes involved and the second process is a kind of watchman, which makes sure that you are doing it properly. That part of it must be taken away, otherwise one ends up being more self-conscious and merely aware that one is concentrating, rather than actually being in a state of concentration. This becomes a vicious circle. Therefore, one cannot develop concentration alone, without taking away the centralized watchfulness, the trying to be careful—which is ego. So the *samatha* practice, the awareness of breathing, is not concerned with concentrating on the breathing.

The cross-legged posture is the one generally adopted in the East, and if one can sit in that position, it is preferable to do so. Then one can train oneself to sit down and meditate anywhere, even in the middle of a field, and one need not feel conscious of having a seat or of trying to find something to sit on. Also, the physical posture does have a certain importance. For instance, if one lies down, this might inspire one to sleep; if one stands, one might be inclined to walk. But for those who find it difficult to sit cross-legged, sitting on a chair is quite good, and, in fact, in Buddhist iconography the posture of sitting on a chair is known as the *maitreya asana*, so it is quite acceptable. The important thing is to keep the back straight so that there is no strain on the breathing. And for the breathing itself it is not a matter of concentrating, as we have already said, but of trying to become one with the feeling of breath. At the beginning some effort is needed, but after practicing for a while the awareness is simply kept on the verge of the movement of breath; it just follows it quite naturally and one is not trying particularly to bind the mind to breathing. One tries to feel the breath—outbreathing, inbreathing, outbreathing, inbreathing—and it usually happens that the outbreathing is longer than the inbreathing, which helps one to become aware of space and the expansion of breathing outward.

It is also very important to avoid becoming solemn and to avoid the feeling that one is taking part in some special ritual. One should feel quite natural and spontaneous, and simply try to identify oneself with the breath. That is all there is to it, and there are no ideas or analyzing involved. Whenever thoughts arise, just observe them *as thoughts*, rather than as being a subject. What usually happens when we have thoughts is that we are not aware that they are thoughts at all. Supposing one is planning one's next holiday trip: one is so engrossed in the thoughts that it is almost as though one were already on the trip and one is not even aware that these are thoughts. Whereas, if one sees that this is merely thought creating such a picture, one begins to discover that it has a less real quality. One should not try to suppress thoughts in meditation, but one should just try to see the transitory nature, the translucent nature of thoughts. One should not become involved in them, nor reject them, but simply observe them and then come back to the awareness of breathing. The whole point is to cultivate the acceptance of everything, so one should not discriminate or become involved in any kind of struggle. That is the basic meditation technique, and it is quite simple and direct. There should be no deliberate effort, no attempt to control, and no attempt to be peaceful. This is why breathing is used. It is easy to feel the breathing, and one has no need to be self-conscious or to try to do anything. The breathing is simply available and one should just feel that. That is the reason why technique is important to start with. This is the primary way of starting, but it generally continues and develops in its own way. One sometimes finds oneself doing it slightly differently from when one first started, quite spontaneously. This is not classified as an advanced technique or a beginner's technique. It simply grows and develops gradually.

The Zen Buddhist Path of Self-realization

Robert Aitken

ROBERT AITKEN *is an apprentice teacher of Zen in Hawaii, serving as leader of the Diamond Sangha and its two centers, the Maui Zendo on the island of Maui and Koko An in Honolulu.*

SOME PEOPLE MEDITATE to quiet their minds, some to get close to God, some to realize who they are, some to develop creativity, some to cure physical illness. A list of reasons to meditate and a corresponding list of meditational ways appropriate for those reasons would more than fill a single article. I propose simply to explore the way that seems appropriate for people who are primarily interested in self-realization.

Self-realization is the experience of seeing into one's own nature and into the nature of the universe. There follows the cultivation and refinement of that vision and its application in the everyday world. This is the path of the Buddha. It begins anywhere, perhaps with the question "What is reality?"

"The Zen Buddhist Path of Self-realization" was written especially for this volume and is printed by permission of the author.

In the Mahayana Buddhist view, reality is a tapestry interwoven of essential nature and phenomena. Essential nature may also be called the Kingdom of God, Nirvana, the Lotus Land, the Primal Void, Buddhanature—the terminology doesn't matter. It is that which is not born and does not die. It is completely empty and has no height, weight, age, color, or form. On the other hand, there is the phenomenal world, which comes into being and inevitably passes away. It is particular and identifiable as man, woman, dog, cat, tree, bush, stone, or cloud—with its own personality and quality. The interweaving of essential nature and the phenomenal world is so intimate that they cannot be distinguished. In fact, they are the same. Hakuin Ekaku Zenji says:

> This very place is the Lotus Land;
> This very body, the Buddha.

The whole of truth is contained in these words, but fine words butter no parsnips. In Zen Buddhism the textbooks consist of dialogues in which the concrete, living fact of these abstractions are communicated.

A monk asked Chao-chou, "Has the dog the Buddhanature or not?"

Chao-chou replied, "*Mu*" ("No" or "Nothing").[1]

Most Zen students start their practice by meditating on this *mu*. What was Chao-chou communicating to his student? Both of them surely were familiar with the statement in the *Nirvana Sutra* that all beings have the Buddha-nature and with the statement attributed to Sakyamuni that all beings actually are the Buddha. Yamada Koun Roshi suggests that perhaps

[1] The Japanese and probably the Tang Chinese pronunciation is *mu*. The modern Mandarin pronunciation is *wu*.

this monk thought Buddha-nature was some kind of possession, like a soul.

"Do you mean to tell me that miserable dog has the Buddha-nature?" Perhaps this was the intent of his question.

Chao-chou's answer, which meant "no" or "nothing" in ordinary Tang Chinese, might seem to be a simple, negative response. But Chao-chou, an accomplished Zen master, was speaking with full awareness of essential nature. His response was not simply from the world of yes and no. It was not, and is not, a cultural concept.

We can gain a glimmer of understanding by recognizing that in Zen all statements by masters are presentations. They are not explanations or interpretations. If you ask an eight-year-old child to show you a fire engine, and he has none, then perhaps he will say, "I don't have one." But if you ask his four-year-old brother to show you a fire engine, you are likely to get an ear-splitting, vocal siren and the roar of the motor, right there in the living room.

Mu, or any word, or any action, or any thing is such a presentation. Our problem is the one that the eight-year-old child has already developed. We are too preoccupied with ourselves, and we allow too much energy to buzz around in our heads, to be able to sense anything directly or to be able to respond directly. Thoughts clog our minds—thoughts of the past or of the future. These are the thoughts that relate to "I," the center of the phenomenal universe. All things serve this "I," even family and friends.

It is this little "I" that is the source of all suffering because it is so important and yet so impermanent— and fundamentally so unreal. Thoughts are its function. When we realize our true nature, when we realize *mu,* our thoughts will be peaks of creativity. But now they are like bells, which, to paraphrase Keats, toll us back to our sole selves.

So first of all, we must learn to handle our thoughts. We cannot block them off. If we try not to think about sex, for example, our minds will be filled with sex. Trying to block such thoughts is simply trying to block ourselves. We are all of a piece.

What can we do? The trick is to divert our energy from thinking to attention. Ordinarily we put energy into planning, remembering, and fantasy. If we channel that same energy into attention, then our thoughts will naturally die down. Ultimately, we reach the point where we are so completely tuned to the object of our attention that nothing is left over—no self-consciousness, no awareness at all of the person who is meditating or working or playing. The usual feedback from our sensory organs that reports, "Knees hurt, back aches, brain is upset . . ." completely disappears. We unite with our practice, whatever it may be, doing *mu,* washing dishes, typing bills of lading, or teaching French.

Mu is the first object of attention of the Zen student,[2] but before he can begin to handle it, he must learn how to concentrate. Breath-counting is the standard exercise of this purpose, not only in Zen Buddhism but in most other religious disciplines originating in Asia as well.

Count one for the exhalation, two for the inhalation, three for the next exhalation, four for the next inhalation, and so on, up to ten—and up to ten again and again. Most people can't do it. Their minds are

[2] A few masters assign "the sound of a single hand," "What is this?" or "Who are you?" as the first theme of meditation.

too busy, perhaps too busy even to reach "one." First things first. Breath-counting should be mastered pretty well before *mu* is attempted.

Regularity is essential. You should have a fixed time. Any time will do, except perhaps right after a meal. When you first get up, just before you go to bed, when the baby is taking its nap—these are good times. When the time comes, you simply go to your cushions and sit down. No decision is necessary.

Similarly, the place should be fixed. Your cushions should always be there, in your meditation corner. A little table to hold incense and a picture of Sakyamuni, Bodhi Dharma, or Kwan-yin will help to create a meditative mood. Your cushions should consist of a soft, square pad, thirty inches or so on a side, stuffed with cotton batting or foam rubber, together with a round pillow, twelve inches or so in diameter. Ordinary square pillows may be substituted. Sit on the pillow and let your knees rest on the pad. You may sit in half lotus, cross-legged with one foot in your lap and one foot beneath your thigh. Or, if you can, sit full lotus, with both feet in your lap. Full lotus is the most secure position. An alternative is to straddle the pillow, placing one knee on each side of it, as your weight rests on your seat, knees, shins, and ankles. You may even sit in a chair, though ultimately your blood will run to your feet, and you may become uncomfortable. Don't try to sit tailor-fashion, with both feet under the thighs—it is impossible to stay erect in that position.

The model for your posture can be that of the maiden who carries a water jar on her head. Her head, shoulders, and hips are on a vertical line, but her spine bends forward at her belt line; her stomach bulges forward naturally; her posterior projects backward; and she is perfectly balanced.

When you first sit down, place your hands in your lap and rock from side to side in decreasing arcs, then from front to back in the same way. This will help you to get firmly settled on your cushions. Then take a deep breath, hold it, exhale, and hold it. Do this a couple of times. This helps to cut the continuity between what you were doing before and your meditation. Then begin your breath-counting. Even if you are working on *mu*, count your breaths from one to ten a couple of times at the beginning of your sitting. Unite with your counting—that is, become each point in the sequence, one, two, three, etc., as best you can.

Keep your eyes lowered, but not closed. They will naturally go out of focus. Various sensations, itching, "good ideas," and even hallucinations may appear. Let them all go by. Pay no attention to them. They are all ego-centered feedback. If you are carried away by thoughts, just bring yourself back. The more you bring yourself back to your practice, the more you develop your capacity to meditate without distraction.

When you can reach "ten" in your breath-counting without losing the count, then you may work on *mu*. Don't wait until your mind is completely clear. The background chatter in your head is only the context of your practice. So long as it doesn't distract you to the point where you lose the count, you are doing well.

The monk who asked the question of Chao-chou was troubled by the existential doubt that troubles us all. "What is that dog?" "What is man?" "Who am I?" "Where am I going?" "Is there any meaning to life?"

And what is the answer? "*Mu.*" What is this *mu?*

Face this *mu*. Pour all your attention into it. Breathe *mu*. Don't worry about whether or not you are doing it correctly. Your anxiety for realization is your correct motivation. Don't think about *mu*, about whether it is this or that. Just do it. Your mind will become quieter and quieter, and *mu* will become more and more intimate. This is the true path to realization.

Be careful to avoid perfectionism. Just sit for a few minutes at first, and don't try to sit more than twenty-five minutes at any time. If you want to sit for an hour, say, get up after twenty-five minutes, walk about, wash your face, and return to your cushions, renewed.

With this practice, you learn to decide, "I will do this; I will not do that." This is not a matter of morality, but rather of proportion. "I will just count this breath, 'one,' and nothing else." "I will devote this moment to *mu*, and nothing else." This decision-making power is carried over into everyday life. "I will now wash these dishes," and if the telephone rings, there is no sense of interruption—it is just that the flow of attention changes. In a discussion you will look at your friend when you speak to him, not out the window thinking of something else, and he will feel related to you. You will concentrate on your work and lose yourself in play, and this faculty for total involvement will then carry over, back into your meditation.

Ultimately, as the *Wu-men Kuan* assures us, you will enjoy a *samadhi* of frolic and play, at the very cliff edge of birth and death. You will be grounded in the realization that you and I are one and the same with the totality of everything, yet also distinctly separate and alone in the vast cosmos, confident and resolute.

Meditation does not stop here. Something is qualitatively different after realization, but it has no value unless it is deepened, refined, applied, and communicated—a lifetime task.

It is said by Krishnamurti and some others that one must discover for himself how to meditate. This is true in some ways, but the Zen teacher is helping his student to get past things he otherwise might spend a lifetime in surmounting. There is no point in having to invent the wheel all over again. Zen training has been worked out through continuing experimentation over 2,500 years, and more. These experiments are still being made, now also in the Western world, and if you are interested, you may participate.

One does need a teacher, however. It is possible to meditate alone or with a friend or group without an experienced leader. But at the point of realization, it is important to have confirmation. The themes of Zen are called barriers in the original Chinese context, barriers in the sense of a checkpoint at a frontier. You must show your ID to the officer in charge. You must show how you stand with yourself and with the universe. False confidence, spiritual pride, and other illusions are very persuasive and require checking by some trusted person. Incomplete experiences may crystallize prematurely without guidance. Moreover, training after realization, by far the most important part of Zen, requires continuing instruction by a qualified master.

Zen Center, 300 Page Street, San Francisco, Calif. 94102, has a list of Zen Buddhist groups and leaders in the United States and Canada, which is available on request. Send them a self-addressed, long envelope with stamp. Counseling by mail is available from the writer of this article, R.R. 1, Box 220, Haiku, Hawaii 96708.

In the process it is good to read. Americans and

Europeans lack the background of Zen Buddhism that an Asian, even a modern Asian, has to some degree. *The Three Pillars of Zen* (Boston: Beacon, 1965), edited by Philip Kapleau, is a good, all-around introductory text, though perhaps one or two of the "realization stories" by Westerners are unnecessarily emotional. *The Zen Teaching of Huang Po* (New York: Grove Press, 1959), translated by John Blofeld, is helpful to more advanced students, though the poetry is rendered in an unduly pedestrian manner. *Zen Flesh, Zen Bones* (Garden City, N.Y.: Doubleday & Company, 1957), compiled by Paul Reps, is a worthwhile reference work, though the last section is really more yoga than Zen. *Buddhism and Zen* and *The Iron Flute,* both by Nyogen Senzaki and Ruth Strout McCandless, are also recommended.

But the important thing is to begin your meditation.

What Is Mu?

Durand Kiefer

DURAND KIEFER *is a retired naval officer, Annapolis '30, who turned to an extensive empirical study of meditation in 1959 after finding that the military and the mystical disciplines have much in common experientially. He has been used as a subject in sensory limitation and biofeedback studies of meditation in a number of well-known laboratories since 1965. He has had no psychedelic drug experience except morphine anesthesia preparation for major surgery in 1945.*

THE STATE OF CONSCIOUSNESS that Arthur Deikman[1] calls trained-transcendent can result from an experience that the Zen Buddhists call *kensho* or *satori*. The characteristics of satori as described by D. T. Suzuki[2] are so similar to those described as the mystical consciousness by Pahnke and Richards[3] in their

This article originally appeared in *Psychologia* 14, no. 2 (1971), and is reprinted by permission of the author.

[1] *Altered States of Consciousness*, ed. Charles T. Tart (New York: Wiley, 1969; Garden City, N.Y.: Anchor, 1972).

[2] *Zen Buddhism*, ed. W. D. Barrett (Garden City, N.Y.: Anchor, 1956).

[3] W. N. Pahnke and W. A. Richards, in *Altered States of Consciousness*, op. cit.

laboratory examination of the experience that the latter may be used as a guide in recognizing the former.

The Zen master Hakuun Yasutani,[4] an eighty-six-
year-old Japanese who has an excellent reputation as
a Zen teacher in both his own country and the United
States, has authenticated, by a brief post-*sesshin* ceremony, the achievement of kensho by several Americans—possibly as many as twenty—during the many
sesshins he has conducted in the United States over
the seven-year period from 1962 to 1969. By his own
account, the depth or completeness of these sesshin-
kensho has varied greatly with the individuals in each
case, and all have been relatively shallow compared
to the maximum transformation of consciousness that
is possible in satori. He has told his kensho students
that their experience with him was more of a matricu-
lation in the school of Zen than a graduation.

Nevertheless, his students who have had this experience describe it in much the same terms as Pahnke
and Richards, but to a variably lesser degree, both in
intensity and in the number of categories experienced.
Some of the characteristics of a Yasutani sesshin were
touched upon in a previous paper, "Meditation and
Biofeedback."[5] Here the sesshin procedure will be described in more detail in terms that might prove useful in a physiological investigation of the process that,
as noted, can result within four to seven days in a
very remarkable revolution in consciousness.

People attend Yasutani's sesshins for various reasons,
but while they are there, the *roshi* considers each person to be a serious student of Zen Buddhism, and he

[4] For a fuller account of the teaching of this master, see Philip
Kapleau, ed., *The Three Pillars of Zen* (Boston: Beacon, 1965).
[5] Published in John White, ed., *The Highest State of Consciousness* (Garden City, N.Y.: Anchor, 1972).

expects him or her to have put aside all other interests and business before arriving at the sesshin, and while there to devote his entire attention wholeheartedly to following the instructions of the roshi, without contention or question. Upon arrival each student is given an instruction sheet that asks him not to read, write, or speak (except to the roshi) or play music during the sesshin, nor to distract other students from their practice by the usual social amenities, and to this end to keep the eyes always lowered so as not to meet the eyes of others or to be caught up in the scene, and in general "to wrap his integrity about him like a cloak" and do nothing to scatter himself or interrupt his single pointed concentration on the learning that he has come to acquire.

At his first *dokusan* (private interview) with the roshi, between five and six o'clock of the first morning, each student is first asked why he has come to the sesshin. The roshi sorts his answer, whatever it is, into one of four general categories and conducts each student's subsequent instruction accordingly. The four categories are (1) to escape the pressure of everyday affairs and repair its ravages to the nervous system, (2) out of curiosity, to learn something about Zen Buddhist practices, (3) out of an intellectual appreciation of Zen philosophy, to learn how to apply it in everyday life, and (4) out of a deep dissatisfaction with ordinary consciousness, to seek or to renew the Zen enlightenment experience, or revolution of consciousness, called kensho or satori.

If the student confirms that he wants kensho and it is his first try (kensho experience is repeatable, usually at greater depth with each repetition), the roshi generally assigns him the *koan mu*, in the form of a *mondo* or Zen parable, based on the question, "Does the dog have Buddha-nature [a soul]?" The roshi makes it very clear at once that no answer that the student can arrive at by thought or imagination is correct, so he must discover some other resource from which to answer, and this is his sole task for the week, or however long it may take. The Zen master thus immediately presents the kensho student with the impasse that ultimately faced the Gestalt therapy patient of the late Fritz Perls.

It is customary for the Japanese Zen master to let each student find his own way of arriving at a non-conceptual solution of his *koan* (test question), whatever it may be, by a process of trial and error that normally takes many years, including many sesshins. In the farewell lecture that closed his last sesshin in the continental United States in October 1969, before his final return to Japan, Yasutani Roshi took the occasion to spell out with unprecedented candor and detail exactly how to "work on" the koan *mu*, to achieve a kensho experience within four to seven days.

The roshi began by saying that the procedure was very simple but very difficult, reminding us that we asked to accomplish something in seven days that ordinarily took ten to twenty years. To do this, the roshi said the student must *become mu* as quickly and directly as possible and maintain this identity for a considerable time (from a few hours to a few days) until teased or shocked out of it by the roshi in dokusan. Yasutani explained:

—That by "becoming *mu*" he meant continuously having no awareness of anything but *mu* at every moment whether awake or asleep, and whether standing, sitting, reclining, walking, waiting, working, eating, evacuating, or whatever.

—That to thus establish *mu* as the total content of consciousness at every instant it was only necessary constantly to repeat the syllable *mu* (moo), silently and rhythmically, with force, determination, and persistence while keeping continuously in mind the question "What is *mu?*"

—That this dual action could be firmly established as a persistent, unconscious habit within three days by forcefully practicing it during the numerous half-hour periods of *zazen* (sitting meditation) every day of the sesshin.

—That this sitting practice of *mu* consisted of keeping the neck and spine straight and vertical while seated with crossed legs on a cushion on the floor (or in a chair with feet flat on the floor) facing a wall about three feet away, with eyes half open and directed at the base of the wall, with hands folded in lap, and with the rest of the body, especially the shoulder yoke, wholly relaxed to gravity except for a conscious tensioning of the *tanden*, or abdominal wall about two inches below the navel, with each exhalation of the breath.

—That in addition to a most energetic persistence in concentration of attention upon repeating the syllable *mu* (aided by the tensioning of the tanden) in a mood of earnest inquiry during zazen periods, the effort to maintain the same degree of innocent, eager attention (called Zen concentration) must be made at all other times while awake, and especially when composing oneself for sleep. The uninterrupted practice of this childlike concentration upon koan exercise is called carrying a koan.[6] (The roshi said that if a

[6] Brother Lawrence and many other notable Christian mystics have called it the practice of the presence of God, and generally —in the beginning, at least—used the Holy Name for their *mu*. See "The Practice of the Presence of God," by Brother Lawrence of the Resurrection, in *The Practice of the Presence of God*, ed. H. Martin (Toronto: Ryerson Press, 1958).

student could carry his koan while falling asleep for the night, he would continue to carry it all night in his sleep.)

—That among the obstacles that make the simple practice of the koan *mu* so difficult, the most common is laziness or simple lack of interest, energy, or determination, and the next is a subtle trick of the ego which substitutes for these a ridiculous mixture of ambition and pride by frequently dangling before the mind's eye the carrot of an imaginary heaven called Nirvana, alternating with elaborate analytical speculations on personal progress toward this goal, complete with erudite diagnoses of one's mental and spiritual state, employing all the psychological, mystical, and esoteric terms in an extensive vocabulary acquired from months or years of reading and talking about Zen and other mystical disciplines. Occasional bursts of actual practice of the prescribed koan exercise are also interrupted for compensatory self-congratulation on such diligence and rapid progress. These very common egotistical preoccupations the roshi calls habit energy, and says they do indeed indicate progress in Zen, negative progress.

—That, on the other hand, if his simple instructions for working on the koan *mu* are adhered to with the three universal requisites[7] of Zen practice—Great Faith (aimless devotion), Great Doubt (earnest inquiry), and Great Determination (desperate persistence)—by anyone, the correct solution of the koan by the realization of kensho experience is "inevitable" within four to seven days. The roshi concluded by citing several dramatic examples from his American ministry.

[7] For a close Christian counterpart, see Evylyn Underhill, ed., *The Cloud of Unknowing*, London: Stuart & Watkins, 1970.

So much for one Zen master's unprecedented exposition of a steep path straight up Zen's nonexistent mountain to the rare peak experience of enlightenment, or ego dissolution.

But what is *mu?*

To an aged student who has taken this master's path a dozen times in a half-dozen years without ever quite reaching the utmost peak, the fierce climb is experienced (in composite retrospect) much like this:

For the first few hours *mu* is a silly syllable, suitable for earnest repetition only by sick cows, and a man feels like a perfect fool, envying the Japanese, whose cows say *maw*, not *mu*. Soon enough, however, one's religious erudition comes to the rescue and he recognizes that "identity with *mu*" and union with God, or with Brahman, or with Tao, or with Allah, are undoubtedly all the same experience with almost identical instructions in the different religious vocabularies for achieving it. So *mu* is God, Brahman, Tao, and Allah—the one Word for all.

This word equation is of no help except to convert the koan practice from embarrassing animal imitation to an exalted form of mantra practice called *japa*, repetition of the Holy Name. For the remainder of the first day it is not too difficult to practice japa with *mu*, occasionally substituting God, Rama, Allah, or even Tao or *om*, with such familiarity that the spirit of inquiry is totally forgotten and the tensing of the tanden nearly so.

Four-twenty zazen the second morning brings a sober return to earnest practice of the triple discipline: *mu*, humble inquiry, and tanden tension. By the end of the day *mu* has become *nada*, a soundless rhythm at the deep level of consciousness in synchronization with exhalation of the breath, only occasionally with tanden tension, as these muscles are becoming fatigued.

Early on the third day the will as well as the body begins to fatigue, and by noon a black frustration from inability to stem the idiot monologue of the mind alternates with a bottomless boredom with the effort to do so. *Mu* is frustration, boredom, and irresistible drowsiness—and nothing else. Unless awakened sharply by the sting of the *keisaku* (the priest's awakening or instant massage stick) on one's own shoulders, or the loud whack of it on a neighbor's, one sleeps fitfully on cushion or chair, jerking awake in terror when he starts to fall over. As pain in legs or back or neck, or all three, fights with drowsiness and fatigue, and frustration fights with boredom as the long third afternoon wears slowly on, *mu* becomes complete misery and remains so until late that evening or sometime the next day, the fourth.

By then *mu* has bottomed-out of misery and become pure, excruciating, exquisite pain, not only general but also particular, usually in a single muscle of the back or one leg. When this particular pain becomes entirely intolerable but is relieved for only a few seconds by movement, there comes a moment when there seems to be no alternative but to "accept" it and live with it motionlessly. At this moment there is a lapse of consciousness that is not sleep, and when it has passed, all pain has gone, and the offending member feels either absent or turned to stone. *Mu* is vast relief and gratitude, shortly turning to a warm comfortable glow "two inches below the navel," where the tanden is effortlessly breathing *mu* without direction at the rate of two or three times a minute, while the entire rest of the body has congealed to stone or simply "fallen off" along with "the mind." *Mu* is the peace that passes understanding, and time has stopped so that it can last forever.

But of course it doesn't. Long after everyone else has gone off to bed or slid into sleeping bags all around the *zendo* (meditation room) floor, the body slowly thaws out and the mind begins to suggest movement and one goes for a long slow walk or lies down and falls instantly asleep. Perhaps, if this peace would simply deepen and endure until it could be presented to the roshi at dokusan, he might test it with a few sharp questions or a few blows and if it survived, convert it to kensho.

There was one sesshin when this miracle of release occurred in the late morning and *mu* was peace all the long day without food and without rest, for it had no appetites at all. But it melted away during the long night, and by morning dokusan, *mu* was again no more than an honest display of the roshi's triple discipline, which won his warm approval and encouragement, as usual, to no end.

And there was another sesshin when the peace of *mu* exploded in a blinding revelation of the absolute sufficiency and perfection of every sense object and the absolute omniscience and infallibility of every sense. But this miracle did not endure the long wait in the dokusan line that day, and again there was nothing for the master to test in the *mu* that was presented to him.

But although the view from only near the top of the nonexistent Zen mountain is not complete, not entirely panoramic, it is still breathtaking, still quite ineffable, and always well worth the climb, no matter how arduous or how often.

But what is *mu*?

When Yasutani Roshi returned to Japan for the last time in October 1969, he left perhaps twenty students and five teachers in America who know. (To know, in Zen, is to be.) For the hundreds of other Americans who seek *mu* now, and for the millions who need to, the answer to Joshu's koan probably lies in America's psychophysiology laboratories, where *mu* is being encountered with increasing frequency in instrumental feedback experiments, under the name of voluntary control of internal states (VCIS).

Christian Meditation

F. C. Happold

F. C. HAPPOLD *is a retired English schoolmaster who has written many books and articles on education, history, religion, and philosophy. They include* Mysticism: A Study and an Anthology *and* The Journey Inwards.

. . . WHILE THE PRACTICE OF MEDITATION has always been present in Christianity, objectives at different periods have not always been the same, nor has the same weight been given to the practice of meditation as a spiritual activity for ordinary people as is given to it in Hinduism and Buddhism.

In Hinduism and Buddhism, and indeed among the Sufis of Islam, the chief object of the spiritual exercises of the Prayer of Meditation at all levels is the deliberate raising and enlargement of consciousness and the cultivation of that superconscious, whereby enlightenment can alone be found. In Christianity, on the other hand, there has been a tendency, particularly since the sixteenth century, to assess the value of medi-

From *Prayer and Meditation*, by F. C. Happold (New York: Penguin Books, Inc.). Copyright © 1972 by F. C. Happold.

tation practices by the extent to which they are conducive to an increase in holiness, whether they make the one who meditates morally a better man or woman. Progress in meditation has tended to be assessed on a criterion of growth in humility and the moral virtues. There has been a tendency among some spiritual directors and writers on meditation to frown on any sort of spiritual exercises which aim at producing mystical states of mind, which are deliberately intended to enable the aspirant to pass into a state of contemplation. If God leads him into such a state, well and good. It must not, however, be sought or expected. This is clearly evident in such classic examples of formal meditation as the Ignatian and Sulpician methods. There does not seem to be any intention that one undertaking the very complicated Ignatian Spiritual Exercises should rise to the heights of contemplation; rather their object seems to be that the sense of sin should be increased. Some of the ways used, for instance meditation on the tortures of hell, in the Ignatian Spiritual Exercises, seem to the present writer truly horrible. One is tempted to wonder what this sort of meditation has to do with the religion of a God of love. In this criticism I would like to avoid any accusation that I do not realize the immense and beneficial effect the practice of the Ignatian Spiritual Exercises has had on men of particular temperament, fitting them for the particular tasks they were called upon to do. There is evidence of their profound spiritual effect on St. Francis Xavier and his companions; and anyone who has read Pope John XXIII's *Journal of a Soul* cannot but have been impressed by the part they played in preparing that saintly man for the great work which fell to him to do at the end of his life. In any case,

St. Ignatius Loyola did not design them for the use of ordinary folk.

Now, while in any comparative study of meditation objectives as found in the religious faiths we are considering, it is necessary to stress this particular bias found among Christian spiritual directors of the West in recent centuries, it would be entirely misleading to create the impression that this bias has been in any way characteristic of all periods of Christian history or is in any way universal. Among the apophatic theologians and spiritual directors of the early Christian Church of the East not only was the objective of spiritual exercises regarded as the attainment of states of illumination and "deification," but also it was believed that by means of these spiritual exercises these states could be reached. Further, the Prayer of Jesus, the "Prayer of the Heart," typical of the deepest meditational practice of the Eastern Orthodox Church, has as its objective that enlargement and elevation of spiritual consciousness which is characteristic of Hindu and Buddhist meditation.

We have noted in some types of Christian meditation the stress laid on the sense of sin. It is desirable to discuss this more fully, since a too great emphasis on, and obsession with, sin can not only be unhealthy but can also lead to mental disorders.

There is a true and healthy sense of sin of the sort that comes to those to whom in one form or other has come the kind of vision of the Holy that came to the prophet Isaiah.

> In the year that King Uzziah died I saw the Lord sitting upon a throne, high and lifted up, and his train filled the temple. . . . Then said I, Woe is me for I am undone! Because I am a man of unclean lips and dwell

in the midst of a people of unclean lips: for mine eyes have seen the King, the Lord of hosts.

Or when it has come as the result of an experience such as that which Warner Allen describes in *The Timeless Moment* and which called from him these words:

Something has happened to me—I am utterly amazed —Can this be that? (*That* being the answer to the riddle of life)—but it is too simple—I always knew it—like coming home—I am not "I," not the "I" I thought— there is no death—peace passing understanding—*yet how unworthy I.* [The italics are mine.]

There is also a healthy sense of sin that arises through the realization of the "fallen" state of mankind and of oneself, of all the cruelty, greed, hatred, intolerance, and consequent misery in the world, the result of ignorance, pride, and preoccupation with self. Or when it arises out of that state of "anxiety" and "guilt," consciously or unconsciously felt by so many in our age and which is characteristic of so much modern literature, in both prose and poetry. For it is only when men feel the sense of alienation, discord, and loneliness that they realize the need of repentance (*metanoia*, a turning round of the mind), redemption, and deliverance from self-centeredness and separation.

Sin, and the feeling of guilt and alienation bound up with it, are realities in human existence, realities not to be shirked.

It is, further, a good and salutary experience to realize one's own littleness and insignificance in face of infinite time and space. Go out on a starlit night. Gaze up at the heavens, studded with stars. Bring to your mind all that modern astronomy has to say about the vast extent of the universe. However much it may hurt, however much you may feel lost and annihilated, let that immensity sink into you, even though it over-whelms and crushes you, and you cry with the Psalm-ist: "When I consider the heavens, the work of thine hands, and the firmament which Thou hast made, what is man that Thou regardest him and the son of man that Thou visitest him?"

What you are doing is meditating on things as they really are. If it ended there, however, it would not be complete. Carry the meditation further and ask the question: "What is there in the nature of man, an in-significant atom of an insignificant planet in an in-significant solar system, that enables him to compre-hend this vast universe, to hold it all in his mind?" And then pass on to the consideration of another not conflicting but complementary aspect, also within the totality of human experience, the sense of some Power upholding it all, a Power that he cannot know through his intellect, but with which man may have intimate communion, and whose nature is Love.

When one has, deep down, realized that the Power behind the universe is Love, one is no longer lonely and afraid. One can trust oneself to it with the sure conviction that upholding it and each one of us are the Everlasting Arms. The sense of insignificance, in-adequacy, sin, and utter unworthiness remains, but the balance has changed.

Above all it is necessary to keep a right balance and a sense of proportion. Not only that; it is desirable also to keep a sense of humor. There is a vast differ-ence between a healthy conviction of sin and inade-quacy and that scrupulosity which solemnizes and mag-nifies every trifle.

> Once in a saintly passion
> I cried with desperate grief,

"O Lord my heart is black with guile,
Of sinners I am chief."
Then stopped my guardian angel
And whispered from behind:
"Vanity, my little man;
You're nothing of the kind."

Perhaps too much space has been given to this obsession with sin that one finds in some types of Christian spirituality. While one of the objectives of Christian meditation is the transformation of character and progress in the way of holiness, it is equally, indeed more so, communion with God through Jesus Christ, the Redeemer, Mediator, and Exemplar; so that one may be able to "put on" Christ, to participate in His Risen Life, to so die to self that one can say with St. Paul: "I live, but it is no longer I, my own little self, but Christ who lives in me." Some have described the objective of the true Christian life as one of becoming "another Christ" (*alter Christus*); and St. Athanasius (in his *De Incarnatione*) penned the words: "God became man that man might become God."

Let us consider some forms that are characteristic of Christian meditation.

THE VALUE OF VISUALIZATION

The Christian faith centers round the Incarnation of Divine Being in a human person, Jesus Christ, and the Christian image of God tends to be expressed in personalistic terms. Consequently one type of Christian meditation makes considerable use of visual imagery. This type of meditation is also found in other religions. While such meditation may perhaps be labeled "lower" meditation, it is of great value and particularly suitable for certain temperaments. Further it has real value as the beginning of a meditation which gradually transcends imagination and visualization and passes into what is essentially contemplative meditation. Types of this sort of meditation are meditations on the Sacred Heart of Jesus, meditations before the Crib or the Holy Child, meditations before the crucifix, icon, or picture, and meditations before the Reserved Sacrament.

COLLOQUY AND AFFECTIVE PRAYER

Colloquy and affective prayer, which is very much of the same character, are two of the most natural types of meditation for ordinary people, and, indeed, for many who have made definite progress in the spiritual life, but who are not able to pass into imageless meditation. In essence, both are a personal conversation with God or with Christ. In them, words, symbols, thoughts, and aspirations combine. They are of value in the simpler forms of contemplative meditation, leading up to the stage when talking stops and one becomes silent, doing nothing except waiting for the still voice of God, speaking in the depths of the innermost being. St. John of the Cross described real prayer as "the privilege of listening for the delicate voice of God."

Nor are colloquy and affective prayer, despite their personal character, bound up with any particular image of God. God may have become the Inexpressible, ungraspable by the intellect, all-pervading Spirit. Yet this Unknowable One, "before Whom words recoil," is by a process of strange, spiritual alchemy, still the Father and the dear Comrade of all our ways. One may say:

You are the Eternal One, Creator and Sustainer of all life, unchanging, unfathomable, beyond human thought and conceiving. Yet I may call You Father and Your Spirit speaks to my spirit. The pure in heart may see You and You reveal Yourself to those who seek You in humility.

A colloquy may spring spontaneously out of a discursive meditation, in which a complex of ideas is intellectually examined. There are a number of colloquies of this sort in the writings of Pierre Teilhard de Chardin. For instance, in *Le Milieu Divin*, Part III, Section 2, "The Nature of the Divine Milieu, the Universal Christ and the Great Communion," a piece of sustained argument culminates in a petition:

> Grant, O Lord, that when I draw near to the altar to communicate I may henceforth discern the infinite perspectives hidden beneath the smallness and the nearness of the Host in which You are concealed.

And then passes into a long colloquy:

> I am beginning to understand; under the Sacred Species it is primarily through the "accidents" of matter that You touch one. . . . What can I do to gather up and answer that universal embrace? . . . To the total offer that is made me, I can only answer by a total acceptance. I shall therefore *react* to the eucharistic contact with the *entire effort of my life*—of my life of today and my life of tomorrow, of my personal life and of my life linked to all other lives. . . . Because You ascended into heaven after having descended into hell, You have so filled the universe in every direction, Jesus, that henceforth it is blessedly impossible to escape You. . . . What I cry out for, like every being, with my whole life and all my earthly passion, is something very different from an equal to cherish: it is a God to adore. To adore: that means to lose oneself in the unfathomable, to plunge into the inexhaustible, to find peace in the incorruptible, to be absorbed in immensity, to offer

oneself to the fire and the transparency, to annihilate oneself. . . .

The colloquy ends with a final petition:

Disperse, O Jesus, the clouds with Your lightning! . . . And so that we should triumph over the world with You, come to us clothed in the glory of the world.

Father Teilhard's *The Mass on the World*[1] is also a sustained colloquy, not coming out of a rational demonstration of a sequence of ideas but out of a particular situation: he found himself in the Ordo Desert without the means of saying Mass. It is one of the most beautiful and moving examples of sustained meditation in the whole of the religious literature of Christendom.

THE PRACTICE OF THE PRESENCE OF GOD

Yet another form of meditation typical of the Christian attitude is the Practice of the Presence of God. The standard book on it is, of course, the one with that title by the little monk, Brother Lawrence, who spent most of his time in the monastery kitchen. It may be defined as the carrying of meditation into the active life, as the holding of the mind, as the duties of ordinary life are carried out, so fixed on God that one is living the whole time in His presence, performing every duty as an offering to Him, in the spirit of the principle so clearly expressed in the Hindu *Bhagavad Gita*:

The world is imprisoned in its own activity except when actions are performed as worship of God [i.e., done in relation to something higher than themselves].

[1] Printed with other pieces in *The Hymn of the Universe*.

Therefore you must perform every action sacramentally, and be free from any attachment to results.

RECOLLECTION

The Practice of the Presence of God is the same as Recollection or the Prayer of Recollection, so well described by Father Thomas Merton:

Recollection makes me present to myself by bringing together two aspects, or activities, of my being as if they were two lenses of a telescope. One lens is the basic semblance of my spiritual being, the inward soul, the deep will, the spiritual intelligence. The other is my outward soul, the practical intelligence, the will engaged in the activities of life. . . .

When the outward self knows only itself, then it is absent from its true self. It does not know its own inward spirit. It never acts in accordance with the need and measure of its own true personality, which exists where my spirit is wedded with the silent presence of the Lord's Spirit and where my deep will responds to his gravitation towards the secrecy of the Godhead.

A Led Meditation on the Lord's Prayer

Frank C. Tribbe

FRANK C. TRIBBE *is assistant general counsel for the U. S. Information Agency. In addition, he is a member of the executive council of Spiritual Frontiers Fellowship in Evanston, Illinois, and is directing a meditation research project for SFF.*

THE LEADER READS:
Dear Lord,
Remove all negative energies and entities from about any of us, and send them to their proper plane; fill them with God's love. Now close the aura of each of us against those and any other negative energies, and in their place put the highest and most powerful vibrations of light, love, and peace. And now, cleanse, clear, fill, and encircle each of us in the white Christ light of healing and protection.
Thank you, Lord. We ask this in Christ's name. Amen.

As we follow the meditation taught by Jesus, we each silently say:
"Our Father Who art in heaven."

"A Led Meditation on the Lord's Prayer" is printed by permission of the author.

And as we hold that phrase in consciousness, we focus upon the pituitary, the master gland, near the juncture of spinal cord and brain—the "heaven" of our own consciousness, with the quality of *being*.

We repeat: *"Our Father Who art in heaven."* (Pause)

Next we express adoration with:
"Hallowed is Thy name."
And as we hold that phrase in consciousness, we focus upon the pineal gland, topmost gland in the brain, between our eyes, our "third eye." This we equate with "mind" and with the Son of the Trinity, the discriminating quality of consciousness. Here we encounter the Universal Mind of God and find the quality of universal *awareness*.

We silently repeat: *"Hallowed is Thy name."* (Pause)

And now we rejoice in the knowing that:
"Thy kingdom is coming, Thy will is being done on earth as it is in heaven."
And as we hold that phrase in consciousness, we focus upon the thyroid—which is the gland of will, situated in our throats between the "heaven" of our heads and the "earth" of our torsos. Here we relate with the Holy Spirit, having the capacity to choose and the ability to bring forth into manifestation, and we encounter the creative forces and find the quality of *creative power*.

We silently repeat: *"Thy kingdom is coming, Thy will is being done on earth as it is in heaven."* (Pause)

Thankfully, we know:
"Thou art giving us this day our daily bread."
And as we hold that phrase in consciousness, we focus

upon the gonad glands, which are our reproductive centers, the transmitters of life, with capacity of creative power. Hence, "bread" is to the creative life of our bodies, the earth counterpart of the "wine," symbolizing the creative forces or Holy Spirit. Since our bread is "daily," we perceive both perseverance and patience or *patient creativity*. Thus, born in each of us is the Holy Child of the New Being.

We silently repeat: *"Thou art giving us this day our daily bread."* (Pause)

Being eternally blessed, we realize:

"Thou art forgiving us our trespasses as we are forgiving those who trespass against us."

And as we hold that phrase in consciousness, we focus upon the adrenals, or solar plexus, where are seated our anxiety syndromes, which may be more deeply perceived as the fear-courage opposites that confront us with the choice to shrink back in alarm or to dare to go forward. Here is found our sin consciousness, and the worry over a sin of omission versus a sin of commission, wherein, ultimately, we hope to find the *courage to forgive*.

We silently repeat: *"Thou art forgiving us our trespasses as we are forgiving those who trespass against us."* (Pause)

And we are so comforted to know:

"Thou art not leading us into temptation."

And as we hold that phrase in consciousness, we focus upon the lyden gland, located in our lower abdomen, and sometimes referred to as the "seat of the soul." Here we sense ego development and ponder the karmic influences of a possible prior lifetime. Though Jesus suggested that self-awareness lies squarely in

the middle of temptation, we can confidently follow
Him to "temptation overcome and karma met" rather
than more sin and guilt. The quality here is *self-
awareness*.

We silently repeat: *"Thou art not leading us into
temptation."* (Pause)

And we gratefully observe:
   "But art delivering us from evil."
And as we hold that phrase in consciousness, we focus
upon the thymus gland, near the heart, with its con-
notations of love, growth, health, understanding, even
of hate, atrophy, illness, and misunderstanding. Herein
we see seated our capacity to react emotionally, and
we strive to avoid reaction to our neighbors with negative emotions. We hope we shall always react with
love, *understanding love*.

We silently repeat: *"But art delivering us from evil."*
(Pause)

And in conclusion we praise by saying:
   *"For Thine is the kingdom and the power and the
   glory, forever. Amen."*
And as we hold that phrase in consciousness, we now
finally focus, in turn, upon:

First, the thyroid, to which "kingdom" relates—it being
the center of will and associated with the Holy Spirit.

Second, the pituitary, to which "power" relates, with
the connotation of authority rather than force, since
the master gland is associated with the Father.

Third, the pineal, to which "glory" relates, with the joy
of a mind universally aware and thus associated with
the Son, the Christ Consciousness.

We silently repeat: *"For Thine is the kingdom and the power and the glory, forever. Amen."* And we reach out to experience further dimensions of reality as we continue our meditation in the Silence. (Fifteen minutes more in silence)

Close (in unison):

Our Father Who art in heaven,
Hallowed is Thy name.
Thy kingdom is coming, Thy will is being done on earth
    as it is in heaven.
Thou art giving us this day our daily bread;
Thou art forgiving us our trespasses as we are forgiving
    those who trespass against us.
Thou are not leading us into temptation,
But art delivering us from evil,
For Thine is the kingdom and the power and the glory,
    forever. Amen.

The Difficulties, Dangers, and Promise

The Difficulties of Meditation

Joel S. Goldsmith

JOEL S. GOLDSMITH *was founder of the Infinite Way Center in Honolulu, Hawaii. Other books by him include* The Infinite Way, The Thunder of Silence, *and* Living the Infinite Way.

IF WE PRACTICE the foregoing meditations faithfully, undoubtedly many questions will arise as to certain procedures in meditation: What about the extraneous thoughts that race through the mind? Should we expect to see visions? Is there a definite length of time for each meditation? How much understanding is necessary? Does diet have any bearing on the effectiveness of meditation? Is any particular posture necessary or desirable?

Let us consider the question of posture first. Meditation is most easily practiced when we are not conscious of the body. If we sit in a straight chair, with feet placed squarely on the floor, the back straight as it normally should be, the chin in, and both hands

"Difficulties" in *The Art of Meditation*, by Joel S. Goldsmith. Copyright © 1956 by Joel S. Goldsmith. Reprinted by permission of Harper & Row, Publishers, Inc.

resting in the lap, the body should not intrude itself into our thoughts. This normal and natural position we should be able to maintain for five, ten, or twenty minutes, without thought reverting to the body.

There is nothing mysterious about posture. In the Orient, few people sit on chairs; therefore, it is natural for them to meditate sitting on the floor with their legs crossed. In that position, they are comfortable; but we, of the Occident, would find such posture not only difficult to achieve, but, for most of us, very uncomfortable to maintain.

If it is remembered that in meditation our whole attention is to be focused on God and the things of God, it will be readily understood that in meditating it is wise for the body to be in a natural or comfortable position, so that the attention is not drawn to the body. The only reason for assuming any particular posture is to make it easier to center the attention on God and to become receptive to Its infinite power. In meditation, a change within the system is noticeable. The spine is erect, the chest is high, the breathing becomes slower, and thoughts race through the mind less and less until they finally cease.

Meditation is a conscious experience. As suggested earlier, it is a great help to begin meditation with some question, thought, or specific idea on which we wish enlightenment. We begin with the idea of receiving an unfoldment from God. If we realize that meditation is a conscious activity of our soul, there will be no danger of our falling asleep or becoming drowsy. Two or three minutes of meditation should be enough to drive away the weariness one sometimes feels at the end of a strenuous day's work. We cannot go to sleep with a mind open, waiting for instruction. Those who fall asleep during meditation fail to make it a conscious experience. At a certain stage of meditation, sleep may come, but such sleep is not a lapsing into unconsciousness. The activity of consciousness would continue during sleep. Meditation is not just a lazy sitting back and saying, "All right, God, you go ahead." It is a quickening alertness and yet it is the "peace that passeth understanding."

Let us be sure there is that peace. We must make certain that there is no strain in connection with meditation. We are not going to take the kingdom of God by force—by mental or physical power. When meditation begins to be an effort, stop it; or we shall defeat our purpose. It is not necessary to meditate for any specific period of time. If the meditation has been of only one minute's duration, let us be satisfied, because if we have been keeping our mind stayed on God for but half a minute, we have started the flow.

Meditation is a difficult art to master. Were it not so difficult, the whole world would long ago have mastered its technique. In my own experience, eight months of from five to ten meditations a day were necessary, before I received the very first "click" or sense of the Presence within—eight months of meditating day and night. Furthermore, I had no knowledge that such a thing as making a contact with God was possible, or that it would accomplish anything once it was achieved. There was, however, deep within me, an unwavering conviction that it was possible to touch something greater than myself, to merge with a higher power. Nobody whom I knew had gone that way before me; nobody had prepared the ground for me. There was only that inner conviction that if I could touch God, at the center of my being, It would take hold of my life, my work, my practice, and my patients. By the end of eight months, I was able to achieve one

second of realization—perhaps it was not even one
second. I do not know how to measure time when it
involves less than a second, but it certainly was less
than a second of realization. It was another week before the next second of realization came and many
days before the third one. A whole week intervened
before the fourth moment of realization was achieved;
then, it happened twice in one day. Finally, the day
came when the realization seemed to last for an eternity and that eternity was certainly far less than a
minute. It was probably three years before I learned
that if I got up at four o'clock, sometime between then
and eight in the morning, I would feel that "click" or
awareness that God is on the field. Some days the
"click" came within five minutes and some days it took
the whole four hours, but never after that did I leave
for my office until the Presence had been realized.

Now there are never less than nine or ten hours out
of the twenty-four given over to meditation—not in
one single period, but five minutes at a time, ten minutes, twenty minutes, thirty minutes. There is no
regular schedule. Sometimes I go to bed at eight
o'clock in the evening, get up at about ten-thirty, and
meditate from then until three o'clock; then back
to bed again until four or four-thirty, up again and in
meditation until dawn. Moreover, whenever anyone
comes to see me, after I have let him talk for a few
minutes, we meditate. This is the way—constant, constant meditation, a constant turning within so that the
inner impulse is kept fresh.

As we advance in this work, if we permit ourselves
to be deprived of our periods of contemplation, by the
pressure of business or the demands of increasing re-
sponsibility, we shall miss the way. Once the Christ-
center has been touched, it is possible that outer activi-

ties may increase to such an extent that they encroach upon the time which should be devoted to meditation. Too great an indulgence in the things of this world might soon take from us the spiritual gift which is infinitely more valuable than any material thing we may sacrifice. The Master withdrew from the multitudes to commune alone in the wilderness and on the mountaintop. We, too, must withdraw from our families, our friends, and our human obligations for those periods of communion necessary to our inner development and unfoldment. An hour or two of meditation or communion, with no purpose or desire of any kind, brings the experience of God to us in an ever-deepening measure.

Frequently the question of diet in relation to meditation is raised. Is there any special diet that, if followed, will enhance one's spiritual capacity? Are certain foods to be avoided by the aspirant on the spiritual path? Should one refrain from the eating of meat?

At every stage of our unfoldment we are tempted to believe that something we do or think in the human realm will help us in the development of our spiritual awareness. This is a false assumption. On the contrary, it is the development of our spiritual awareness that changes our everyday habits and mode of living. As the aspirant progresses along the spiritual path, he may find himself eating less and less meat and, ultimately, may reach the point of being unable to eat any meat at all. Let us not, however, believe that there is virtue in some act of omission or commission, that some form of material sacrifice will increase our spirituality. Spirituality is developed through the reading of spiritual literature, the hearing of spiritual wisdom, the association with those on the spiritual path, and through the practice of meditation. The kingdom of God is found by inner realization. The outer transformation in one's dietary habits is a direct result of an inner spiritual grace; it is a result of the spiritualizing process taking place in consciousness. Abstaining from the eating of meat is not a means of developing inner spiritual grace; but the development of inner spiritual grace leads to the renunciation of such things on the outer plane.

Another question that arises is in regard to psychic visions. Are such manifestations a desirable or necessary part of the experience of meditation? Psychic visions, such as seeing colors or being confronted with an apparition of a supernatural character, may have some relevancy to our human experience, but remember this: they are entirely on the psychic level or in the mental realm of consciousness. In spiritual literature, these visions are never referred to or considered as spiritual experiences. Psychic experiences have nothing to do with the world of Spirit. The psychic world of seeing visions, colors, or anything of that nature is left behind in the realization that right here and now we are spiritual beings, the manifestation of all that God is. For that reason, let us not linger in the psychic realm, but rise above it into the pure atmosphere of Spirit.

Many times in meditation we attain a sense of peace or harmony—the realization of the presence of the Christ. These are inspiring experiences, but we must be willing to give up even that deep peace and rise to the next higher level of consciousness in which the attaining of that peace is of no significance or importance whatsoever. Having realized the everpresence of the Christ, is it necessary to have any kind of an emotional reaction? Whether we feel emotionally satisfied or emotionally starved will make no difference, since we shall have realized that the activity of the Spirit is an eternal thing, always with us.

One of the greatest hindrances to meditation is the fear that we do not have enough understanding with which to begin this practice. The Psalmist forever disposed of such fear and doubt when, in Psalm 147, his heart and lips sang forth the praises of God: "Great is our Lord, and of great power: his understanding is infinite." It is *His* understanding, not ours, that is important. Let us give up all this nonsense about our not having enough understanding or about our having such a great understanding. We must remember, it is *His* understanding. In quietness and confidence, therefore, let us turn within to let truth reveal itself. There is no limit to understanding, if our dependence is on God's understanding rather than on our own. There is not a person reading this chapter who does not have sufficient understanding to begin the practice of meditation and, thereby, enter the kingdom of God. By grace, even the thief on the cross was enabled to enter paradise "this day," and we, too, by grace can enter the gates of heaven at this very moment.

The major difficulty with meditation is, of course, the inability to hold the thought in one direction. This is neither your fault nor mine, but is partially the result of the accelerated tempo of modern living. The infant is given a rattle, and as soon as he outgrows that he is given another toy. His entire attention from infancy through adolescence and into adulthood is centered on people and things, so that if he ever found himself alone, he would be overcome by fright. Most people have never learned how to sit down by themselves and be quiet; many of them have never learned how to be quiet long enough even to read a book. Our culture has focused attention on the things of the world to such an extent that we have lost the capacity to sit quietly and ponder an idea.

When we close our eyes in an attempt to meditate, we are amazed to discover a boiler factory inside of us. All sorts of thoughts flash through our minds, simple things such as: Did I disconnect the electric iron? Did I turn on the refrigerator? Did I put the cat outside? Other thoughts, not so simple or unimportant, come in—thoughts of fear or doubt. Let us not be afraid of these thoughts; they are world thoughts. We are like antennas picking up all the broadcasts of the world. If we disregard these world thoughts, in a few days or weeks they will die for lack of feeding. Only as we accept them as our thoughts, do we feed them.

Although our object is to attain a quietness and receptivity, we should never try to still the human mind; never try to stop thinking or to blank out our thoughts. It cannot be done. When we begin to meditate and thoughts of an unruly nature come, we should remember that they are world thoughts, not our thoughts. Let them come. We will sit back and watch them, see them impersonally. Eventually they will stop and we will be at peace. As often as our thought wanders in meditation, we gently come back, with no impatience, to the subject of the meditation. There will come a time, as we continue in this practice, when these extraneous thoughts will not impinge on our consciousness. We will have starved them by neglect. We will have made ourselves so unreceptive to them by not fighting them that they will not return to plague us. But if we fight them, they will be with us forever.

In meditation we must be very patient in our endeavor to conquer any sense of unrest. No truth that we do not already know is going to be given to us from without, but the light presented on that truth from within our own soul makes it applicable in our experience. Truth that comes from without is a mere semblance of truth; it is the truth revealed within our own consciousness that becomes the "light of the world" to all who come within range of it. "I, if I be lifted up from the earth, will draw all men unto me." Meditation will lift us to the point where we apprehend the word of truth in its inner significance. The rhythm of the universe takes possession of us. We do not move; we do not think; but we feel that we are in tune, that there is a rhythm to life, that there is a harmony of being. This is more than peace of mind; this is the spiritual peace which passeth understanding.

In order to enter into the mystical life, we must master the ability to remain in the silence without thought. This is the most difficult part of all spiritual practice. In no way is this a cessation or repression of thought, or an effort toward such; instead, it is such a deep communion with God that thought stops of its own accord. In that moment of silence, we begin to understand that the divine Mind, or Cosmic Consciousness, is an infinite Intelligence imbued with love, and It functions as our being, when conscious thinking has been stilled.

In our everyday life, we may have one plan in mind and the Cosmic Mind may have another, but we shall never know Its plan so long as we are busily engaged in thinking, scheming, and reacting to the activities and distractions of the world. To receive the divine grace of the Cosmic Mind, there must be periods when the human mind is in a state of quiescence. The individual who is master of his destiny has reached the state of consciousness where nothing in this world is of any importance to him. Only that is significant which takes place when he has risen above the sea of thought. In that high place the divine thought, the divine activity of consciousness, reveals itself. This does not mean that our mind must or will become a total blank, but it does mean that throughout the day and night we must have several periods of time in which there is no desire other than the joy of communion with God. It is in this complete stillness and respite from thinking that the Father takes over in our experience.

Before we can enter the mystical life, the habit of continuously thinking and talking must be transformed into the habit of continuously listening. Our Master spent much of his time in silent meditation and communion, and we may be assured that he was not asking God for anything of a material nature. He was not talking; he was listening. He was listening for God's direction and instruction, for God's guidance and support.

It is in developing that listening ability and receptivity that the human mind is quieted and becomes stilled to such a degree that it is an avenue or instrument through which God manifests and expresses Itself. This human mind, this reasoning, thinking mind, is not to be put off or destroyed. It has its place. It is not consciousness, but it is a facet of consciousness, an avenue of awareness through which we receive knowledge and wisdom from consciousness.

Thinking is an initial step leading toward meditation. Let us suppose that we are not advanced to the place where we live in a constant state of receptivity. True, God is always uttering His voice, but we are not always listening. Thought may be used to help us reach that exalted state of listening consciousness, but in meditation no thought should be used in the sense of an affirmation or denial.

Let us suppose that we desire to meditate, but the human mind is in such a turmoil that we do not find ourselves immediately in a state of quiet and peace. Instead of attempting to blank the mind and blot out these disturbing thoughts, we use the mind and turn to scripture or to some other book for inspiration. Now let us see how this operates in the use of such a quotation as "Be still and know that I am God." The student who has learned to rely on affirmations would repeat over and over again, "Be still and know that I am God. Be still and know that I am God. Be still and know that I am God," until he reached a point of self-hypnosis and, in that state, temporarily found himself still. To repeat continuously, "Be still and know that I am God," is nothing but suggestive therapy, nothing but affirmation and denial used to hypnotize oneself. It is not spiritual practice; it is not spiritual power. Some people have become so hypnotized through the use of such an affirmation that they actually believe that they, as human beings, are God.

Now let us take that same statement, but instead of using it as an affirmation, let us discover its real meaning through meditation:

"Be still and know that I am God." What does that mean? Of course, you know, Joel,[1] that you are not God. So what does this mean? It says, "I am God," not that Joel is God. That is quite different. I, yes, "I and the Father are one. . . . God in the midst of me is mighty. . . . I and the Father are one." Yes, Joel and I, the Father, are one. The Father and Joel are one; right where I am, God is—closer than breathing, nearer than hands or feet. Be still, Joel, because the I in you is God. You do not have to seek protec-

[1] The reader may insert his own name in using this meditation

tion, help, or healing anywhere. I am with you. Be still and know that that I is your protection, your salvation, your security.

In the contemplation of this scriptural passage, peace enfolds us and we are at rest in a divine stillness.

A few on the spiritual path achieve this stillness quickly and easily, but for most, the way is long and difficult. It is not for any of us, however, to boast about the rapidity of our progress nor to decry its slowness, but to pursue the way with steadfastness and unswerving purpose. Most of us have periods of gradual progression, punctuated by interludes of desolation, when we feel that we have lost the way and are wandering in a maze of conflict and contradiction. Often we find that, after these valley experiences, we go forward to new heights where unsuspected vistas spread out before us.

There are a few gifted individuals who, because of previous experiences, have been so well prepared that their way seems to be much easier than others'. The purity of consciousness that they have developed makes the ascent into spiritual consciousness a beautiful, gradual, and harmonious journey beset with very few problems.

For most of us the path is up and down, but by the end of a year or two there is usually a feeling that we are a trace ahead of where we were the year before. The prerequisite for the hearing of the still small voice, for the actual experience of the Christ, is to prepare ourselves by study, meditation, and mingling with others on the spiritual path. When we hear the still small voice within us, we have received God's grace and the purpose of meditation is being achieved.

We dare not be satisfied with anything less than the

experience of God Itself. It is the pearl of great price. It is for each of us to decide how much time and effort will be given over to meditation: to determine whether we will spend a few spare minutes now and then or so arrange our lives as to permit prolonged periods of uninterrupted quiet in which to contact the inner Presence and Power. The years necessary to the study and practice of meditation are not years of sacrifice to the aspirant; rather are they years of devotion to that which is his goal in life. It requires patience, endurance, and determination, but if the realization of God is the motivating force in our lives, what the world calls a sacrifice of time or effort is not a sacrifice, but the most intense joy.

Meditation as Metatherapy

Daniel Goleman

DANIEL GOLEMAN, Ph.D., *earned his doctorate in psychology at Harvard, where he investigated meditation as a means of coping with daily stress. From 1970–72 he studied and practiced meditation in India, where he met many Indian yogis, Tibetan lamas, and Buddhist monks. Mr. Goleman's articles have been published in* Journal of Transpersonal Psychology, Biofeedback and Self Control 1971.

PEOPLE WHO MEDITATE have long recognized in themselves and in fellow meditators marked improvement of their psychological state and of psychosomatic disorders. For ages the books of wisdom of the East about meditation have been used as guidebooks for changing one's state of consciousness. But only recently have scientific studies begun in the West of the psychophysiological processes involved in meditation, dreaming, and related areas which help us understand the therapeutic and consciousness-altering effects of meditation.

This understanding is aided by bridging the gap between East and West in terms and concepts. The Indian novelist Raj Rao writes in *The Serpent and the Rope*, "Destiny is nothing but a series of psychic knots that we tie with our own fears." He could have added that those "psychic knots" that shape our destiny are tied also with our hopes, plans, fantasies, ruminations, desires, aversions, memories, daydreams, reflections. For destiny is what in the East would be called *karma*, the consequences of our past deeds and thoughts, and these psychic knots *sanskara*, the accumulated contents of our mind which interact to determine the way we live each and every moment of our lives. Karma does not need lifetimes to play itself out, as is the common belief; the Buddhist *Abhidhamma* teaches that birth and death is a process that takes place in every moment of our life, and the law of karma is at work in the mind's moment-to-moment transmigration.

Karma and sanskara work the same everywhere but are understood differently from time to time and place to place, just as each culture slices reality in its unique way. A concept similar to karma is the fundamental assumption of psychological thought: that past experience determines present behavior. All of Western psychology deals with the intricacies of sanskara and karma, but under categories like "defense mechanism," "self-system," "cognition," "motivation," "conditioning"—all the technical names we have for the psychological processes that form the aggregate called "I."

The Western psychologists I find most useful in seeing how sanskaras determine our destiny are thinkers like Wilhelm Reich, Fritz Perls, Alexander Lowen, and Al Pesso. These men see the mind and body in terms of the psychophysiological principle that every change in physiological state is accompanied by an appropriate change in the mental-emotional state, and conversely, every change in mental-emotional state is accompanied by a physiological change. Mind and body are one interacting whole; as one changes, so does the other. Through reading musculature—the way one stands, moves, holds oneself—the Gestalt or bioenergetic or psychomotor therapist gets to the major psychological issues in a person's life. Events that may seem in the main emotional or mental are consequential physiologically: tears and laughter matter both to body and to mind.

As a person is shaped by the events of his lifetime, his nervous system is the repository of all experiences of emotion, strain, pleasure, fatigue, excitement, tension, stress, etc., whether of "physical" or "mental" origin. It is as though the organism were a rope that continually accumulates sanskaras like knots, knot upon knot, in one massive Gordian knot. New sanskaric knots—tensions—are tied every time the organism is impinged upon by the day's events. The more tied up—that is, up tight—one is, the more the day's events will impinge, and so the more new tensions one will get. There are miniscule tensions (the anticipation while waiting for a hot fudge sundae) and small tensions (the anxiety of dodging taxis while crossing Times Square) and still bigger tensions (the acute anxiety of taking a crucial exam for a promotion or college entrance). Most of psychotherapy deals with big sanskaras, or tension complexes, like the Oedipus struggle, sibling rivalry, and adolescent identity conflict. One of the largest sanskaric knots known is the "double-bind," where a child continually gets contradictory messages of both love and hate from its mother, which may destine the child for schizophrenia.

We all have sanskaras, but each of us has a different

and unique set, just as we each have our own life history. In terms of the Western psychologist's way of seeing things, the sum total of these sanskaras is "personality" or "character structure"; to the yogi they are karma. To the psychologist some sanskaric tension states are functional and some are not; to the yogi no sanskara is desirable. For both the yogi and the psychologist the issue is the same: how to untie these psychic knots, how to reduce the accumulation of tensions.

Attachment or ego involvement—letting things get to us—is the root cause of the tendency to acquire tension. With nonattachment the experiencing of the hot fudge sundae or the menacing taxi or the exam is all the same: noted, dealt with, but no tension is evoked by the event, and where there is no tension, there will be no new sanskaras. Or if sanskaric knots are made, they will be of the kind that untie themselves with the gentlest tug—that is, come out in dreams or in meditation.

MEDITATION AND DREAMING

Studies of sleep and dreaming show that in sleep, gross body movements build up to a peak just before the onset of dreaming, terminate abruptly with the onset of the dream state, and reappear when dreams stop. Dreams occur while the body is not moving; while we are shifting around during sleep, there is little dreaming. Gross body movements inhibit dreaming. But while we dream, our body makes very fine, slight movements. If someone is awakened while dreaming and asked what he was dreaming, the action in the dream will correspond to these slight, abortive muscular stirrings.

If a person is deprived of dream-time by being awakened every time he gives signs of dreaming, and if this continues night after night for several nights, he will begin to show signs of mental illness: heightened tension, anxiety, irritability, difficulty in concentrating, impaired co-ordination, and so on. He will also make increasingly frequent efforts to dream. When allowed to dream, he will dream much more until the lost dream-time is made up. If, on the other hand, he is deprived of the same amount of *non*dream sleep, none of these things will happen to him.

Since before Freud people have recognized that the content of a dream—especially on the level of action—derives in part from the residue of recent days' events or from major events in the dreamer's remote past. Each of these events has left its imprint. What happens in dreams, and what causes those slight muscular stirrings, is that the body is releasing tensions accruing from past life events. In dreaming, tensions or sanskaric knots are undone by being released on the level of nerve and muscle, out of the awareness of the dreamer. He need not recognize the event being played back and is unlikely to accumulate more tensions, being totally relaxed at the time.

Any single set of muscular stirrings may represent the release of tension from many different life events, or they may be only one small part of the work the body must do to free itself of the residue from a single past moment of trauma. The function of dreams, as Barbara Lerner, of the Chicago Neuropsychiatric Clinic proposes, is to maintain the organism as a healthy unit by readjusting to a state of integration parts that have become dysfunctional during waking activities. Normally, enough tensions gathered during the day are undone at night so that we can bear to go out again the next day and gather some more.

Physiological studies of people meditating by Harvard Medical School's Herbert Benson and others have shown a reduction in basal metabolism—blood pressure, breathing rate, oxygen consumption, heartbeat, etc.—*greater* than in deep sleep. Meditation requires that the body be held immobile, and as in dream-sleep, muscle activity drops to a minimum level. During meditation the body is in the state of deep relaxation and physical immobility resembling the state in sleep prerequisite to dreaming. And in fact the body seems to undergo a process similar to the tiny movements that accompany tension release in dreaming. When these movements occur in meditation, they are not experienced as a dream, but rather as spontaneous movements and internal sensations: momentary or repeated twitches, spasms, gasps, tics, hallucinoid feelings, sexual excitement, jerking, pressures, heat, and the like. These movements and sensations are completely spontaneous and unintended.

The "dance" that each part of the body does in meditation seems to be the undoing of all those day-to-day dances that have left their mark on it in the past. The particular dance done in meditation is different for each person and could be interpreted as a function of the unique set of tensions he carries with him. The amount of such dancing is inversely proportional to the length of time one has been a meditator: toward the beginning movements are intense; the longer one has meditated, the less frequent they are. Virtually every school of meditation recognizes this phenomenon, and though the terminology varies widely from system to system, most all see it as cleansing or purification, the erasure of accumulated tension or sanskaras.

If indeed these movements in meditation serve the same function as in dreaming, it may be that through meditation the meditator would automatically free himself of those legacies of the past that psychoanalysis deals with. But in meditation the process would occur on the physiological level rather than the verbal, and would deal with a scope of sanskaras far wider than are touched upon in psychoanalysis.

MEDITATION AND BEHAVIOR THERAPY

Meditation may also bring about changes at the level of action and thought, in much the same way as do behavior therapies. The behavior therapy technique most closely resembling meditation is "systematic desensitization" as developed and practiced by Joseph Wolpe and Arnold Lazarus. Systematic desensitization involves three principal operations: (1) training in "deep muscle relaxation," relaxing in sequence the various muscle groups throughout the body until the whole body is thoroughly relaxed, (2) the construction of an "anxiety hierarchy," a systematic list centering on a particular problem or situations in any way distressing to the patient, listed according to the degree of anxiety elicited by each (the patient is taught to visualize a vivid image for each item in the hierarchy), and (3) presenting each item in order, paired with the state of deep muscle relaxation. The list is ascended item by item, each item being presented until it elicits no anxiety, at which point the next item is presented. If the problem is fear of dogs, for example, the hierarchy might go from the weakest item—the thought of a cocker spaniel—to the strongest—"walking by a growling police dog." At each therapy session the patient first becomes deeply relaxed, then imagines the weakest item until it evokes no anxiety at all, and proceeds through the list toward the strongest. Finally, no item evokes anxiety. When the patient then finds himself in a real life situation with a growling police dog, he will feel none of his former fear (although he will maintain a healthy caution).

In the early stages of meditation there is a state of peaceful absorption and relaxation where "inner speech"—all the mentative activities of the mind—are still at work. In this state the whole contents of the mind can be seen as composing for the meditator a "desensitization hierarchy." The contents of this hierarchy are organic to the life concerns of the meditator; they are drawn from the stored pool of his total experience. This hierarchy is inherently self-regulating: the organizing principle for item presentation is, literally, "what's on your mind," and so optimal salience is guaranteed.

As in desensitization therapy, the hierarchy is "presented" in meditation coupled with a body state of deep relaxation. Because items are not presented so systematically as in behavior therapy, meditation is a slower and less efficient means to the same end. But unlike the therapy, desensitization in meditation is not limited to those items that a therapist and his patient have singled out as problematic (though these are certainly included) but extends to all phases of experience, to whatever comes to mind. Meditation can be seen as natural, global ("whole person") desensitization.

MEDITATION AND ANXIETY REDUCTION

Recent research into the biochemistry of anxiety by Washington University's Ferris Pitts, Jr., has shown that anxiety symptoms and attacks can be induced by infusions of lactate, a normal product of cell metabolism in the process by which cells break down glucose and extract energy from it. Studies at UCLA of metabolic changes during Transcendental Meditation found that lactate decreases markedly at the beginning of meditation and continues to decrease during meditation. After meditation it remains at a low concentration.

This metabolic side effect of meditation is reflected in the meditator's day-to-day life. Even someone who has just begun to meditate regularly can notice that immediately after each meditation he is not so likely to respond to people or situations in a tense way—he is relaxed, calm, and can take things as they come. With prolonged practice of meditation this relaxed stance toward life's vicissitudes pervades the meditator's day. He finds himself reacting with equanimity where once he would have gotten angry, paranoid, envious, greedy, titillated, or whatever reaction his particular personality makes him susceptible to.

The deep relaxation the meditator gains in meditation stays with him through the day as the physiological slowing down and alteration of his metabolism infuses with his waking activities. The longer he has meditated, the more his waking metabolism will resemble the deep rest and relaxation of meditation. Tension accumulates most heavily when there is anxiety, and relaxation is the direct physiological opposite of tension. The meditator, cooled out by meditation, gets fewer new tensions than once he would have. The normal tendency to accumulate tension in moments of anxiety is countered by a new tendency: to stay relaxed. Relaxation is naturally coupled with any troublesome life situations in a process of *in vivo* desensitization.

MEDITATION AND SEEING THINGS AS THEY ARE

Our usual habits of perception might more accurately be called misperception: not seeing what we look at, not hearing what we listen to, not feeling what we touch, not noticing what we attend to. These habits are in part the result of our mind's moment-to-moment transmigration. Our ordinary train of thought is endless, stops nowhere, and has no destination. At every moment it kidnaps our awareness, keeping it from raw sensory experience. As you read this, for example, you've probably spent some mind moments eating, buying something, visiting your favorite place, or doing whatever it is your mind wanders to when it's not being here, now. Three major perceptual factors governed by the mind's wanderings are "habituation," "selective inattention," and "selective perception."

Habituation is the tendency to notice only what is new to us, and once it has become the old and familiar, to see it no longer as it is, but rather as we have cataloged it. Habituation is characteristic of the ordinary waking state—for example, we don't really see the places we pass by daily on the way to work except in a stereotyped manner. Studies of Zen meditators in Japan, however, found that during meditation there was no habituation. One Zen master said of this state of mind that it is one of "noticing every person one sees on the street, but not of looking back in curiosity." To the degree that the awareness gained in meditation transfers to waking state, habituation is replaced by a new habit of seeing all things—even old things—as new.

Selective inattention, as propounded by the psychiatrist Harry Stack Sullivan, is the tendency to "fail to recognize the actual import of a good many things we see, hear, think, do, and say." This failure of recognition protects us from the anxiety that would be evoked by confronting the actual import of those things—for example, "failing" to see an amputated beggar as we pass by on the street. Selective inattention is a means for minimizing anxiety in our lives. But with meditation anxiety becomes increasingly reduced regardless of what surrounds us in the external world. Consequently, the meditator can allow himself a wider scope of attention as the avoidance of anxiety becomes less and less an operating force in his life.

While selective inattention is a failure to see what would make us anxious, selective perception is the tendency to perceive the object of our desire to the exclusion of other things. A man who is starving notices food, whereas a man who is sexually aroused notices women, though both food and women may be present. The object of our desires becomes figure and all else becomes ground. In this sense, our desires create our universe. Desires and drives, however, loose their hold on the meditator as the anxiety states which empower his deficiency needs become rarer. With this process the tendency to selective perceptions would fade and the visual gestalt would no longer be divided into figure and ground to spotlight objects of desire.

A further force in meditation's control of the wandering and distracted mind is the practice it provides in "one-pointedness." Virtually all meditation techniques involve focusing attention on one object, whether that object be a sound, a visual image, or a bodily sensation, to the exclusion of all other objects.

At first most meditators find themselves *not* attending
to the meditation object far more than they attend to
it. Gradually this changes. A habit of easy concentration develops to replace the normal "mad monkey"
pattern of frenetic changes to which Marshall McLu-
han referred when he said, "Our mind is a magazine
with a new edition every four seconds." With continued concentration no new editions are forthcoming,
and deep absorptions can occur which lead the mind
to experiences discontinuous with normal states of
consciousness. The transfer effect of one-pointedness
in the waking state may be to facilitate full attention
to each successive moment of awareness freed from
distractions. When through meditation one has overcome the tendency to habituation, selective inattention, and selective perception, and has become practiced in one-pointedness, one would tend to meet each
moment of experience wholly, completely, and with
unbiased perception.

MEDITATION AND ALTERED STATES OF CONSCIOUSNESS

In its later stages meditation acts much more directly to free one to meet each moment wholly. The
habits that form our day-to-day lives are to a large
extent shaped through intermittent reinforcement by
brief moments of satisfaction and pleasure. The proto-
typical experience of the moment of satisfaction is
the baby's bliss at its mother's breast. For us now that
moment is sought from any number of persons—boss,
parent, teacher, friend, lover, spouse—and in a wide
array of actions—work, sex, eating, buying, hanging
out. The payoff moment is felt as an inner satisfaction
and is experientially always basically the same, although

the situation in which it occurs can take myriad forms, often fleeting and unpredictable.

These gratification moments are a basic unit of reinforcement in our day-to-day lives. They are most strikingly evident in the "neurotic cycle," where they give partial cessation of anxiety which leads to the repetition of self-defeating acts and the reinforcement of crippling neurotic defenses. In the same way, in what might be called the normal cycle, intermittent gratification moments lead to the repetition of daily activity patterns and the affirmation of one's role and self-identity. The ego can be seen as a system for attaining maximum gratification moments. Our motivations, whether oriented toward achievement, affiliation, or power, are likewise strategies for gaining gratification moments, the payoff for any and all social games.

Keith Wallace has proposed a "fourth major state of consciousness" on the basis of brain wave and physiological changes observed in laboratory studies of meditation by himself and others, such as Joe Kamiya at the University of California Medical Center in San Francisco. This state of consciousness has been known to practitioners of all schools of meditation for millennia, and is sometimes called *samadhi*, a *jhana*, *satori*, or simply "the void." In this state ego, time, and space are transcended; it is described as being felt as the essence of that same gratification moment: peace beyond bliss. But in the fourth state gratification is attained without recourse to any of life's social games and is pure and prolonged rather than distracted and fleeting.

Initially the fourth state comes only while one is absorbed in meditation. With further practice, the fourth state changes in metabolism, brain wave activity, and the experience of ongoing essence-of-bliss seems to accompany participation in waking activities. Every moment is as satisfying as the next: when there is eternal gratification, waiting for a hot fudge sundae is fully as satisfying as eating it. So is not getting it at all. With the integration of the fourth state into waking activity, the "fifth state" emerges, where what was once a peak experience becomes a plateau. No activity need be pursued any longer simply in the hope of a gratification moment. People and things can be seen and dealt with free of the compulsion to use them for self-gratification, since the state of nongratification that feeds the compulsion has vanished. The chain of attachment to people, social role, and activities is broken. Equanimity prevails.

Fifth state detachment centers one in the self and liberates one from dependence on any source outside the self. Actions can become guided by the highest motivation, what the late psychologist Abraham Maslow called metamotivation, as opposed to "deficiency motivation" or "being motivation." In deficiency motivation, for example, one eats out of hunger; in being motivation one eats out of the desire for tasty food; in metamotivation one is beyond even the desire for tasty food and can eat solely according to bodily needs. So with all activity in the fifth state: the consciousness guiding action is unclouded by deficiency or desire, and so can act for the good of all concerned, free from self-interest.

At this point the meditator reaches the state Erich Fromm describes as enlightenment, where "he who awakes is open and responsive to the world, and he can be open and responsive because he has given up holding on to himself as a thing, and thus has become empty and ready to receive. To be enlightened means the full awakening of the total personality to reality."

When one has reached this point, Western psychology no longer is adequate to understand him, for our psychological theory is based on and generated by beings who are in this sense "asleep," not "awake." Western psychology has never had a sampling of beings of the sort described by Fromm, or by the Buddha in the *Dhammapada*: "He whose mind is not whetted by lust and not affected by hate, who has gone beyond both good and evil, for him, the Awake, there is no fear."

MEDITATION AS METATHERAPY

For most all of us there is lust, anger, and fear from time to time. For some people, those who dwell in the psychic space called hell, where the world is seen through a negative lens, there are these feelings much of the time. Most of us spend most of our time in a psychic space of "normal neurosis" which could be called so-so land—not so great one moment, feeling good the next, our mood vacillating as much as our mind. Very, very few live in the psychic space of the enlightened, "the other shore," where there is fearless, clear perception, peace beyond bliss. Therapy is a rescue operation, retrieving people from the hell realm to normal neurosis. Dreams are a natural, built-in device for doing the same thing. But meditation can save us even from normal neurosis and carry us safely to the other shore.

One limit to therapy's effectiveness is that although in therapy one may be freed from past tensions, nothing is done about the *process* of tension accumulation itself. Thus the patient may no longer have nightmares about (or because of) his mother, but may start to have them about his therapist. And the therapist who has undergone years of analysis to free himself

from the tyranny of his own childhood is not pre-
vented from severe depression when, for example, his
teen-age son or daughter runs off to Morocco to smoke
hashish. In therapy the effects of old sanskaras are undone, but the process whereby they accumulate continues, albeit in a new pattern. Therapy may afford
a degree of freedom from the past, but it cannot ensure freedom from the future.

The work of freeing the meditator from his sanskaras seems to proceed on three levels: a body-level
approximation of psychoanalysis; desensitization of
thoughts as they arise during meditation; and desensitization of troublesome life situations as they are met
in a state of low anxiety. In these ways meditation
may serve as a "therapy." But the effects of meditation
extend beyond those of therapy—for example, to improving normal perception through limiting the influence of habituation, selective inattention, and selective perception in the meditator's day-to-day life,
and by giving practice in one-pointedness. And by taking the meditator through the fourth state to the fifth
state of consciousness, it can give him a wholly new
experience of himself and the world which can liberate
him from the compulsion to pursue people and activities for self-gratification. In this sense, meditation
is metatherapy.

On his path the meditator incidentally undergoes
those changes therapy aims for, but these personality
and behavior changes are subsidiary to the meditator's
goal. He seeks not to alter his behavior, but to alter
his state of consciousness.

Only now are experimental studies being conceived
and designed that bear on the effects of meditation
for waking state activities. A day may come when in-

stead of recourse to the old model of therapist, patient, and psychopathology, troubled people will turn to a new method and model: meditation teacher, meditator, and the road to higher states of consciousness.

Meditation: The Dangers and Rewards

Haridas Chaudhuri

HARIDAS CHAUDHURI, PH.D., *is professor of philosophy and president of the California Institute of Asian Studies in San Francisco. His books include* Integral Yoga, Philosophy of Meditation, *and* Mastering the Problems of Living.

MEDITATION HAS COME THESE DAYS TO MEAN many things to many people. At the time of the Buddha, or even before him in the Upanishadic period of ancient sages, meditation was an all-out search for the ultimate meaning of life. It was the methodology of deepening value-consciousness and higher self-realization. But nowadays it is in the process of being converted from the art of higher living into a technological device. The more it is looked upon as a technique, the more it loses its spiritual significance and degenerates into a value-empty mechanism.

Depending upon one's unconscious motivation, meditation can be used as an escape from reality or as a means of regression. It can be used as a passage to the

"Meditation: The Dangers and Rewards" was written especially for this volume and is printed by permission of the author.

land of lotus eating or as a flight to cloud number nine. But under competent and mature guidance, it can also be used as the art of authentic self-realization or as an exciting adventure in consciousness in search of limitless truth.

Broadly speaking, there are three kinds of meditation: conventional, unconventional, and creative.

CONVENTIONAL MEDITATION

The ultimate goal of conventional meditation is peace of mind or soul. Meditation is like a boat for crossing the river of life—a river frightfully agitated with emotional storms and ideological conflicts.

The method is one-pointed concentration on a particular metaphysical or mystical system of concepts and values. The guru explains this system and emphasizes its absolute validity. The disciple looks upon the guru as a divine personality and consequently accepts his message as the supreme truth.

The main technique here consists in shutting out from view disturbing ideas, thought vibrations and suggestions, and distracting emotional waves. The constant repetition of a mantra, a concise sound symbol of the accepted value system, is a powerful instrument for focusing attention upon one's article of faith or for building up a mental fortress against all intruding and alien forces, whether external noises or incompatible thoughts or distracting inner urges and impulses.

The mantra may have a manifest meaning such as "May I be united with God" (or with the Buddha or Christ, etc.) or "I am one with the Supreme Being" (or cosmic consciousness," etc.). I have discussed some helpful mantras elsewhere.[1] The mantra may not have a manifest meaning as in the case of a sound formula like *Ok ad da phat* or *Pung tang meng*. But since man is a thinking animal and since the thought process—like nature—knows no vacuum, even the mantra that is seemingly most meaningless instantly and unconsciously acquires a meaning in the mind of the meditator. It becomes meaningful as the vehicle of the power of truth communicated to him by his guru. So indirectly it would symbolize the entire value system for which the guru stands.

The use of a mantra may be accompanied by the use of a *yantra*, or visual image. By visually reflecting upon the same value system, the *yantra* reinforces the effect of the mantra. It may be the image of the guru or of the guru's guru or of the guru's chosen deity (*istadevata*) or his accepted value system. The mantra and the *yantra* together can successfully finish the job of desensitizing the mind to all alien thought systems and of transplanting the mind from one cultural system to another.

In other words, the traditional or conventional mode of meditation produces the condition of monoideism, to use an expression of William James, which serves as a safe anchor for the meditator. Lifted out of the tumult and turmoil of conflicting social forces, the meditator experiences profound peace and a wonderful feeling of liberation. He enters into the kingdom of heaven within the golden shell of his own psyche.

But a heavy price is unknowingly paid for the transcendental bliss of conventional meditation. It involves the suppression of one's independent thinking, resulting in incapacitation for critical evaluation of the

[1] *Integral Yoga* (London: George Allen, 1970).

value system handed by the guru. No thought structure or value system can possibly express the absolute truth, for the simple reason that it represents a certain degree of abstraction, as Korzybski would say, from the infinite fullness of concrete reality.[2] Unthinking identification with a particular value system may produce a wonderful sense of bliss, and that is perhaps all some people are capable of attaining—at least in this life. But such an identification also closes one's mind to the vastness of the real and confines it within a conceptual prison house. It produces, no doubt, some amount of liberation from worries and anxieties, but it also provides an escape from authentic freedom of thought and direct contact with the multidimensional Being. Providing an escape route from one kind of thought system from which the meditator felt alienated, it binds him hand and foot in another thought system—occultist, supernaturalistic, metaphysical, or mystical. The latter may be more glamorous and exciting, but is nonetheless hypnotically binding.

Since the guru is considered a God-man in the conventional practice of meditation, another side effect of meditation is a greater or lesser degree of emotional fixation upon the guru. When this emotional fixation is complete and permanent, a tragic atrophy of the disciple's personal growth takes place. If the guru is mature, he would of course take it upon himself to liberate the disciple in due time from his hypnotic spell. But an immature guru would naturally be inclined to perpetuate the situation for his personal glory or ego satisfaction.

[2] A. Korzybski, *Science and Sanity*, 4th ed. (Lakeville, Conn.: International Non-Aristotelian Library, 1962).

UNCONVENTIONAL MEDITATION

Meditation in its unconventional form is the art of systematic questioning. It encourages the habit of constantly asking questions—questions put to reality and questions put to one's own self. It is radical thinking.[3]

Unconventional meditation is energetic protest against naïve acceptance and blind acquiescence in tradition and authority. It is an act of rebellion against the prevailing scale of values and pattern of thinking. It is a breach with the life of immediacy, whether instinctual (the immediacy of animal spontaneity) or fatalistic (unthinking conformity).

Unconventional meditation unfurls the banner of negative freedom and devastating criticism. It lays major emphasis upon the elements of doubt and scrutiny in man's search for truth. Plato called it "divine discontent." Whether it eventually succeeds in arriving at any positive vision of truth is a different question. It primarily takes delight in shaking the foundations of traditional life and society and in performing the operation of intellectual surgery.

The principal method of this type of meditation consists in raising such radical questions as these: Who am I? Am I really what society takes me to be? Am I a string of social labels and designations? Am I a collection of assorted social masks and fixed roles? Race, religion, nationality, sex, complexion of the skin, social prerogative or deprivation, public adoration or condemnation, glory of success or humiliation of failure— do these really reflect the inmost essence of my being? Does any of them singly or all of them collectively

[3] Haridas Chaudhuri, *Philosophy of Meditation* (New York: Philosophical Library, 1965).

constitute my essential reality? If not, who am I? And whither am I going?

Preoccupied with these radical questions, unconventional meditation is inclined to discount the value of such traditional techniques as repetition of mantra on a fixed formula, contemplation of *yantra* or traditionally interpreted visual image, or worship of a guru accepted as the divine-made-flesh, or emotional exuberance with the aid of chanting and dancing and singing, or adoration of a holy scripture as the revelation of absolute truth. All of these, in ultimate analysis, amount to a king-size devotional lollipop. They produce the magical effect of profound mental peace by protecting the ease-loving, peace-seeking mind against the harsh realities of the world by drugging it against hazardous challenges of personality growth. These are, of course, time-tested techniques of hypnotizing the mind into a dreamland of unspeakable bliss. But can there be any mature growth except through the baptism of fire?

At times the hardly audible voice of the innermost soul rings in the ears. Is it better to be a child satisfied in the Disneyland of colors, sounds, and sights than a Socrates dissatisfied in his critical search for the unseen and the unknown? Is it better to be a ritualist content with the canned food of religious ecstasy than a Buddha seized with the divine discontent in his renunciation of luxury and power?

There are very potent drugs available today to serve as delightful substitutes for the former. But unfortunately, there is no substitute for the latter.

CREATIVE MEDITATION

Meditation in its unconventional form does indeed perform intellectual surgery. It purifies the spirit in man and paves the way for optimum growth and self-perfection.

But in order to reach the ultimate goal, the full circle must be completed. In our search for truth we may begin with conventional meditation. This is the spiritual kindergarten. But one must advance further and forcefully shake loose from all emotional bonds. The religious life of unquestioning faith, the devotional life of the immediate absolute, must be followed by metaphysical protest and intellectual catharsis. The protective shell of peace, happiness, and transcendental bliss guaranteed by the guru must be broken with the thrust of radical doubt and criticism. The illusions of unconscious wishfulness must dissolve like soap bubbles in the rushing wind. This is the rebellion stage of advanced growth. Following the dialectic of inner evolution, the affirmative stage of infancy must be followed by the negative stage of doubt and denial, protest and rebellion, catharsis and critical analysis.

But in order to enter upon the final phase of spiritual maturity and full blossoming of the human potential, one must further advance to the point of negating negation and transcending transcendence. This gives rise to meditation in its most mature and creative form.

In the course of mature meditation, critical reasoning is consummated in all-embracing truth-vision (*prajna*). This is what Sri Aurobindo has called comprehensive, supramental, or integral consciousness (*vij-*

nana).[4] Ancient sages of India described it as the vast truth consciousness (*satyam ritam vrihat,* or *rita-cit*).[5] It is mature enlightenment resulting from deep concentration (*nididhyasana*) upon the inmost center of one's own existence or upon the ontological root of one's own being.

One-pointed concentration purified by the baptism of fire awakens the transpersonal Being-energy, which lies dormant at the center of every human being's psychosomatic system. It is the psychonuclear energy oriented to the supreme value-consciousness of truth, beauty, love, and freedom. Ancient sages described it as the mystic fire. Yogis experience it as the celestial serpent *kundalini,* darting with lightning speed through the spinal cord toward the summit of consciousness (*kailasha*). As it reaches the height, the light of cosmic consciousness is kindled in all its effulgence, and the thousand-petaled lotus of cosmic love blossoms to the full.

Cosmic consciousness at its most sublime is what yoga disciplines call the transcendent Being-cognition (*Brahma-jnana*). In the light of supreme truth a mature yogi or *rishi* (seer of truth, sage) is in a position to reaffirm everything that was rejected before. Rejection itself is now rejected on the basis of one's grand affirmation of the positive truth-vision. Every little fragment of truth is freshly revealed just as it is in respect of its proper essence, function, and cohesion in the total scheme of cosmic evolution.

Briefly stated, the language of total truth-vision in which meditation is culminated runs somewhat like

[4] *The Synthesis of Yoga* (*On Yoga I*) (Pondicherry, India: Sri Aurobindo Ashram, 1957).

[5] Sri Aurobindo, *The Life Divine* (New York: E. P. Dutton, 1953).

this: Mantra is a help, but beyond a certain point it becomes a hindrance. Visual symbol is a help, but beyond a certain point it becomes a hindrance. Reason is indeed a great help, but beyond a certain point it becomes a hindrance. The guru is no doubt a great help, but beyond a certain point he may become a hindrance. So the mature guru withdraws at the right time with a loving act of sacrifice, just as the mature mother does when her child grows up.

Let us conclude by saying that meditation is the inner process of psychic evolution brought to the focus of self-consciousness in man. Intensification of consciousness (*tapas*) produces the awakening of the mystic fire, the transpersonal Being-energy, the latent divinity in man. A dynamic interplay between the self-conscious ego and the transpersonal Being-energy eventually results in mature enlightenment or integral awareness of the true Self as a unique focus of Being on the one hand and a creative center of planetary evolution on the other. Freely creative self-expression in the best interest of mankind is the result of integral Being-realization.

Meditation and Psychic Phenomena

Daniel Goleman

Nothing whatever is hidden;
From of old all is clear as daylight.
—from the *Zenrin*, lines composed after *satori*

WE HAD JUST FINISHED TWO MONTHS of intensive practice of a Southern Buddhist meditation technique in
the town of Bodh Gaya, the site of Buddha's enlightenment under the bo tree and the main place of pilgrimage for Buddhists the world over. Nearly one hundred Westerners had crowded into a semi-abandoned
Burmese monastery there for a series of consecutive
ten-day meditation courses, meditating four to twelve
hours a day. No reading, no writing, minimal talking,
no smoking, no leaving the monastery, no music—
only meditating. After finishing five ten-day sessions
we were relaxed, high-spirited, and eager to venture out
into the world. A bus was arranged to take twenty-five
of us the few hundred miles to Delhi, from where we

"Meditation and Psychic Phenomena" originally appeared in
an abridged form as "Psychic Phenomena and Eastern Meditation" in *Psychic*, June 1973. Copyright © 1973 by Daniel
Goleman and printed by permission.

would scatter throughout India, Nepal, Ceylon, or back to the West.

Among those on the bus was Ram Dass (formerly Richard Alpert, Ph.D., of Harvard's psychology department), back in India for his second time. On his first trip he had encountered a highly revered yogi of indeterminate age (estimates vary from the seventies to well over one hundred—no one knows anything certain about his origins)[1] who wandered freely over most of India, especially the north. Called simply Maharaj-ji, he was venerated for his qualities of compassion, detachment, simplicity, and humility—not his psychic abilities. He almost always wore a heavy woolen blanket—but little else—whether in the hot sun of the plains or the icy cold of the Himalayas, saw to it that everyone who came to see him was fed, had no possessions but the clothes he wore, and continued to lead the unpredictable and timeless life of a wandering yogi, even though people throughout India wished him to stay put, preferably in their village.

When Dr. Alpert first met Maharaj-ji, he was not impressed; indeed, on first meeting he was quite skeptical. The next day at their second meeting, however, Maharaj-ji quite out of the blue mentioned that some nights before, Alpert had been out looking at the stars and had begun to think about his mother, who had died the previous year—all of which was true. When Maharaj-ji then went on to specify that Alpert's mother had died of a disease of the spleen, something broke within the skeptic, and he found himself sobbing uncontrollably. Maharaj-ji became Alpert's guru, had him study raja yoga in a temple in the Himalayas, gave him the name Ram Dass, and finally sent him

[1] Maharaj-ji died in late 1973. *Editor.*

back to America to share what he had learned with others.

After two years, Ram Dass was now back for more teachings from Maharaj-ji. But Maharaj-ji was proving elusive: Ram Dass had been in India six months, and no one had any idea where Maharaj-ji might be. He could be anywhere. Ram Dass's plan, after the Bodh Gaya course, was to find him.

Our bus slowly made its way down the highway to Delhi. The throngs of cows, children, bicycle rickshas, and bullock carts that swarmed over the road made twenty mph seem a top speed. In the late afternoon of our second day out of Bodh Gaya we entered the ancient city of Allahabad. There at the Prayag, where the three holy rivers of the Ganges, the Yamuna, and the mythical Saraswati meet, an amazing spiritual gathering had convened: the Kumbh Mela.

A few days before our bus left I had made my own two-day expedition by train to reconnoiter the Kumbh, a month-long meeting of millions of devout Hindus who gather there once every fourteen years to bathe at the sand flat where the sacred rivers meet. It was the most awesome assemblage I had ever seen. A vast city of tents housed countless wandering yogis, swamis, and others who devoted themselves to the spiritual life. Some of these yogis never left their caves in the Himalayas or their jungle retreats except to attend these gatherings, and everywhere on the vast grounds of the Kumbh were yogis sitting naked meditating for hours in a circle of fire under the hot sun, or marching in religious processions, or singing holy songs day and night.

So impressed had I been by my short visit that as we approached Allahabad, I directed the bus off the main road to the edge of the city where the rivers meet.

But as we pulled onto the sand flat, we found it was totally deserted! Where a few days before there had been millions of people, now there was no one: the Kumbh Mela was over.

Remembering an intriguing old temple on the edge of the flats, I directed the bus toward it, hoping my companions would find it of some interest and not be too disappointed about the vanished Kumbh. As we pulled up to the temple, someone looked out the bus window, did a double take, and then shouted, "Hey, there's Maharaj-ji!" And there he was, wrapped in his blanket, standing with another man by the side of the road and laughing as the bus pulled to a stop.

We later learned from his companion, a university professor at whose house Maharaj-ji had been staying, that about an hour before, Maharaj-ji had insisted that a ricksha be found and they both go across town to that temple—a place Maharaj-ji rarely visited. He gave the professor no reason, but was emphatic that they do it at once. But when they got to the temple, Maharaj-ji did not go in, suggesting instead that the professor get some tea for himself at a nearby tea stall. Then abruptly Maharaj-ji said they should leave the tea stall at once, and the two of them arrived at the temple just as the bus pulled up. At that moment Maharaj-ji said to the professor, "Here they come!"

How does Maharaj-ji do it? No one knows for sure, but some acknowledge his ability to tune into events in distant time and space as an attribute of the state called *sahaj samadhi*—the "easy state" or enlightenment. A person in this state has surpassed the distinction between the normal waking state and sitting in meditation. He is in a receptive, meditative state all the time, his mind calm and quiet in the midst of all his activities. One by-product of reaching this plateau of meditation in action, it is said, is the attainment of *siddhis,* or supernormal psychic powers.

The connection between proficiency in meditation and psychic abilities is recognized in Patanjali's *Yoga Sutras,* written about fifteen hundred years ago. This classic statement of yoga theory spells out how when one attains perfect concentration in meditation, a range of supernormal powers becomes possible. A partial list of the powers enumerated in the *Yoga Sutras* includes knowledge of the past and future, understanding of all languages, knowledge of one's past lives and of the nature of another's mind, the ability to become invisible, precognition of the moment of one's own death, superhuman strength, and the supernormal abilities of hearing, touch, sight, taste, and smell.

While studying in Bodh Gaya I was shown the *Visuddhimagga,* an ancient Buddhist treatise on meditation, dating from the period of the *Yoga Sutras,* which describes in great detail how to perform a range of supernormal feats, among them virtually every psychic phenomenon studied by modern scientists. This document stresses that a prerequisite for performing these feats well is the mastery of *samadhi*—total stillness of mind and perfect one-pointed concentration— a factor also emphasized in the *Yoga Sutras.* The feats themselves, however, are to be done not during *samadhi,* but rather while the mind is in a semi-stilled state just after coming out of *samadhi.* The extreme difficulty of mastering the mind to the degree required —so that one can still the mind totally at once, whenever, wherever, and for however long one wishes— makes *samadhi* a very rare achievement.

The directions in this Buddhist meditation manual for psychic abilities are reserved for a later part of the training in the techniques of Buddhist meditation. They are to be tried only after the pupil has undergone experiences (e.g., the nirvanic state) that lead to ego loss. They are referred to as concentration games, and not much is made of them. Those who play them never talk about them. An Indian teacher told me about a pupil of his, a sixteen-year-old girl in Calcutta, who made rapid progress in meditation. He claimed she developed the ability to appear in two places at once, but after a while lost the ability. Apparently it is hard work to attain and maintain this kind of ability.

The directions are also quite clear and seem reasonable enough, provided one has the required mental agility to meet the minimal requisite: a totally stilled mind. For example, the instructions for remembering one's past lives (assuming one believes he has any past lives) are as follows:

First, emerge from the state in meditation of a totally calmed mind. Then turn your attention to your most recent act—sitting in meditation—and review all the happenings during the session in reverse order, i.e., from most recent to most distant.

Then review in reverse order all the acts of the day that led up to meditating. All this memory is normal, but in this state it will be especially easy.

Then review in the same way all the past days, weeks, and years of your life, through life in the womb, back to the moment of "rebirth-linking," when your being entered your present body, back to the moment of death of your previous body.

This moment of death is especially difficult to recall, and it may be necessary to revert again and again to the state of totally stilled mind just prior to trying to recall the rebirth-linking.

When there arises knowledge of rebirth-linking, then

memory of one's past births in reverse order is available, including details of name, race, appearance, experiences of pleasure and pain, and how one died in each birth, back through endless eons of world expansion and contraction.

Buckminster Fuller, speaking from general systems theory's view of the world, points out that our senses are designed to limit what we can perceive. Among the things we cannot directly perceive with our senses are electric, magnetic, and radioactive fields, and colors in the ultraviolet range. But the greatest limitation in our sensory apparatus is that we cannot tune the *flow* of the events from which our universe is concocted. Existence is continuous, unbroken, no matter how our senses and language-directed attention may seem to segment reality. Because of this, says Fuller, "99 percent of the transactions of the universe are infra or ultra to man's tuning." What we think of as psychic abilities seem to represent a more subtle sensory tuning to the total interrelatedness of nature and events in the universe than most of us manage. The *Visuddhimagga*, in its instructions for psychic feats of whatever sort, invariably starts with a normal faculty— such as memory, sight, or hearing—which is then deepened in potency by combining it with intense concentration.

Purifying "the doors of perception" is a goal of meditation: transcending the self-limiting effect of one's habitual self-image, sensory patterns, and manner of "cutting the reality pie." If the meditator succeeds, he expands his ability to tune into the flow of the world around him. A parapsychologist might see that retuning in terms of increased psi ability.

No parapsychologist has ever reported testing a yogi of the stature of Maharaj-ji, and "experienced" Western meditators are, by Eastern standards, mere beginners. One paradox of psychical research is that those countries most prepared scientifically to test psychic phenomena are Western and industrial, and no longer have the spiritual traditions and disciplined "schools" that reportedly produce highly self-transcendent and retuned beings. Those nations with such schools and their "graduates"—who are most likely to perform impressive psychic feats as subjects—are neither culturally nor economically likely to test them.

However, Dr. Jamuna Prasad, a psychologist working with the Indian Institute of Parapsychology in Allahabad, India, is now conducting a study of paranormal powers manifested during yogic training. At the Menninger Research Foundation in Topeka, Kansas, biofeedback researcher Dr. Elmer Green has conducted studies with Swami Rama, a forty-eight-year-old yogi who began training at age four. Swami Rama showed unusual ability to control his bodily functions, including brain waves, heartbeat rate, and skin temperature. While in Stage Four sleep (theoretically "dead to the world"), Swami Rama was able to perceive conversation going on in the room which he accurately described later.

In every Eastern spiritual tradition that teaches how to acquire supernormal sensory abilities, these teachings are always accompanied by stern warnings that such powers are not to be displayed for personal gain or fame, but should be used sparingly and only for the good of others. Their misuse is damaging to spiritual evolution; it is not the power that matters, but the purity of being of the person who possesses it.

In Buddhist tradition, for example, there is open recognition that supernormal psychic faculties arise incidentally out of proficiency in meditation. But these are not the meditator's goal. He is on the path to a higher realization: nirvana. The Buddha and his close disciples are said to have possessed such powers, and Buddhist scripture often tells of his using them for the sake of those who demanded signs and wonders. Still, he deplored their use, preferring to spread his teaching through the power of its intrinsic truth. In the Buddhist view, one who embarks on concentration exercises to obtain supernormal powers as a goal in itself is doing so with the wrong motivation and at great danger to himself. If power corrupts, supernormal power can corrupt superlatively.

Still, unbelievers throughout the ages (and to the present day) have demanded signs and wonders, and often these demands have been satisfied. Perhaps the largest single body of reports of psychic phenomena is found among the lore of the world's religions, in accounts of the lives and deeds of mystics and saints. One of the striking aspects of these tales of psychic feats is their remarkable similarity, no matter how distant in historical epoch or culture the men who perform them. Compare, for example, the *Visuddhimagga* recipe for supernormal memory with the following passage from *The Way of the Pilgrim*, a nineteenth-century Eastern Orthodox account of a pilgrim's constant meditation on the Prayer of the Heart:

> The human soul is not bound by place and matter. It can see even in the darkness, and what happens a long way off, as well as things near at hand. Only we do not give force and scope to this spiritual power. We crush it beneath the yoke of our gross bodies or get it mixed up with our haphazard thoughts and ideas. But when we concentrate within ourselves, when we draw away from everything around us and become more subtle and refined in mind, then the soul comes into its

own and works to its fullest powers . . . there are people who see light even in the darkest of rooms, as
though it streamed from every article in it, and see
things by it . . . and who enter into the thoughts of
other people.

Fifteen centuries before the pilgrim wandered
through Russia, the Desert Fathers had taken to the
Egyptian desert to practice the same meditation on
Jesus through constant repetition of the Prayer of
the Heart. Accounts that survive to this day of the
daily life of these Christian hermits mention many
miraculous events and psychic phenomena. St. Je-
rome's fourth-century biography of St. Paul the Her-
mit (died c. 347), for example, recounts that one day,
"as St. Antony himself would tell, there came suddenly
to his mind the thought that no better monk than he
had dwelling in the desert. But as he lay quiet that
night it was revealed to him that there was deep in the
desert another better by far than he, and that he must
make haste to visit him."

Setting out with no clear destination in mind, Je-
rome recounts, Antony begins a journey through un-
charted desert in which animals appear to him to give
him signs directing him to the hidden retreat of Paul.
Paul greets Antony with the words "From old time, my
brother, I have known that thou wouldst come to me,"
and since his own death is imminent, Paul tells Antony
that he has been sent by God to bury him. Paul adds
a request that Antony, "unless it be too great a trouble,
go and bring the cloak which Athanasius the Bishop
gave thee, to wrap around my body." Antony, amazed
that Paul should have known of the cloak and Athanasius, set off at once on the three days' journey to his
own cell to fetch the cloak. On the second day of his
return trip, Antony had a vision of Paul "climbing the

steps of heaven," and knew that Paul had died. On reaching Paul's cave, he found the lifeless body still kneeling as if in prayer.

The Desert Fathers were the early Christian equivalent of yogis. For thousands of years and up to the present, yogic lore has been replete with tales of psychic phenomena. Yogananda, an Indian yogi who lived and taught in America until his death in 1952, tells many such occurrences in his *Autobiography of a Yogi*. The story of Yogananda's grand-guru Lahiri Mahasaya's first meeting with Babaji, his master, resembles the meeting of St. Antony and St. Paul. One day while walking through the hills of the Himalaya, Lahiri heard his name called. Following the voice, he came upon a hidden cave where Babaji was waiting for him. Babaji told him that in his past life Lahiri had lived in that same cave and had been Babaji's disciple. Lahiri stayed there with him for ten days and then returned to his regular life as a government civil servant, but from then on Babaji would appear to him in moments of need.

Yogananda also tells of similar feats by his own master, Sri Yukteswar, a disciple of Lahiri. One day Yogananda was to meet Yukteswar, who was to arrive on a train from Calcutta at 9 A.M. At 8:30, however, Yogananda received a telepathic message that his master would not be on the train. Telling a friend about it, Yogananda stayed at home, while his scoffing friend went to the station to meet the nine o'clock train. While Yogananda sat in his room alone, the form of Yukteswar appeared before him, telling him that the rare experience of witnessing a materialization such as this was a special boon granted Yogananda, and that if he went to meet the ten o'clock train, Yukteswar would be on it. Yukteswar also described specific details of his future arrival at the train station, and then vanished. Yogananda, rushing to the station to meet the ten o'clock train, met his friend who reported that Yukteswar had not been on the nine o'clock. But when the ten o'clock train pulled in, Yukteswar was on it as predicted, and every detail was as described.

Stories of Tibetan yogis are also replete with psychic wonders. The biography of the eleventh-century Naropa, for example, echoes both Antony and Yogananda in recounting how Naropa first met his own successor, Marpa. One morning while meditating, Naropa saw a sphere of bright light and then a vision that his disciple-to-be was presently staying in India with a certain novice monk at a monastery in Pullahari. Naropa at once sent a messenger to summon Marpa to him. The meeting of Marpa and Naropa fulfilled a prophecy that Naropa's own guru, Tilopa, had made to him, that his successor would come to him from that same monastery at Pullahari.

The teaching lineage of Tilopa, Naropa, and Marpa is unbroken to this day. One of those links is Chogyam Trungpa Rinpoche, presently teaching meditation and Buddhism at centers in Barnet, Vermont, and Boulder, Colorado, and in many major American and Canadian cities. The stories of Rinpoche's birth and discovery as the eleventh incarnation of a *tulku* (a being who consciously chooses to be reborn, often to complete unfinished spiritual work) show that psychic ability was not only relatively common in Tibet of this century, but also built into the functioning of its huge monasteries. Every important monastery had among its bureaucratic posts that of *srungma*, or oracle, whose precognitions would come while in a trance.

The tenth Trungpa tulku had been the supreme

abbot of Surmang, one of Tibet's largest monasteries. On his death in 1938, the Surmang lamas sent an envoy to Gyalwa Karmapa, the head of their sect, to inquire if he had any indication where the reincarnation of the tenth Trungpa might be. After some months Karmapa had two visions, and was able to tell the lamas that the Trungpa tulku had been born in a village five days' journey north of Surmang, the name of the village sounded like *Ge* and *De*, the family had two children, the door of the family's house faced south, they had a large red dog, the father's name was Yeshe-darge and the mother's Chung Tzo, and the son, who was almost a year old, was the eleventh Trungpa. A party of lamas set off at once to find him, and after five days' travel arrived at the village of Geje where, after a search, they found the baby boy in the family and surroundings predicted. From that time on Rinpoche was raised by the lamas to take his rightful place as head of the monastery. His formal training in meditation and other spiritual disciplines began when he was five.

In his autobiography *Born in Tibet*, Rinpoche reports the regular use of psychic abilities in the form of ritualized divination (*tagpa*) in Tibet. He does not go into any detail in describing how the divination is done, but treats it on the one hand as nothing special, and on the other as something to be resorted to only in times of genuine and urgent need. While leading a party of several hundred Tibetans fleeing the Chinese Communists across the high and trackless Himalayas to India, Rinpoche himself undertook *tagpa* to determine such things as whether the Chinese were lying in wait along a chosen route and, when lost, which direction to take.

Given the large body of reported instances through

the ages and in the present day of meditation-linked psychic phenomena, how does Western science evaluate these claims? Professor Alex Wayman, of Columbia University, suggests in a review of the religious meaning of altered states of awareness that Western scientific disbelief of reports of these kinds of events may be in large part "judgments made simply through skepticism of any abnormal powers of mind, refusing to admit those powers when the researcher himself lacks them." Still, increasingly greater numbers of Western researchers are taking these phenomena seriously and subjecting them to rigorous study.

The most thorough study of meditation and ESP in the West to date was conducted over a three-year period by Karlis Osis and Edwin Bokert, of the American Society for Psychical Research. Their report, "ESP and Changed States of Consciousness Induced by Meditation," appears in *Journal of the American Society for Psychical Research* 65, no. 1 (January 1971). Testing ESP ability directly after people had finished meditating, the one factor they found to be most strongly correlated with ESP was "self-transcendence and openness"—the key quality that marks a successful meditator.

The psychiatrist Arthur Deikman has described two styles of relating to the world, one an action mode oriented toward manipulation of the environment, the other a receptive mode where the world is engaged with openness, harmony, and acceptance. The receptive mode—typical of early infancy—is made possible in adults through meditation, which brings about what Dr. Deikman calls deautomatization, an undoing of usual ways of perceiving and thinking. With our habitual sensory censors and perceptual biases removed, we are in a position of expanded tuning, where the world can tell about itself.

It is among people who are deautomatized and open to the world, Osis and Bokert's study suggests, that we would expect to find high psi ability: Zen masters, Indian yogis, and Tibetan lamas.

For us in the West, psychic phenomena are novel, mysterious, and fascinating; for masters in the great meditation traditions, these same occurrences are taken as ordinary, matter-of-fact, and even trivial. Maharaj-ji, for example, never mentions his psychic abilities; he merely uses them from time to time, with the same casualness he might show in asking if you had enjoyed your lunch.

The fifth-century Buddhist meditation manual I read in Bodh Gaya sets down the recipes for supernormal sensory powers in as detailed and prosaic a manner as an automobile owner's manual describes the workings of the engine—and yet these phenomena are included as an aside, as secondary to the system of spiritual development of which they are side effects. One critical difference between Eastern and Western approaches to psychic phenomena is that for the East they are seen within a spiritual and religious context, whereas for the most part the West approaches them from the extremes of "the occult" or as experimental laboratory phenomena.

To put psi in the foreground as an end in itself seems to be neither spiritually helpful nor the best way to go about producing it. According to Osis and Bokert, "willing" ESP actually inhibits it, just as making an effort to produce alpha waves has been found self-defeating. Psi seems to belong to the category of acts handicapped by our usual manipulative mode of relating to the world. It may be that learning to "not do" is a key to psi ability, and meditation is the most direct training in not doing. If we change our being in this way, psi ability may come of itself.

One lesson for us from the meditation traditions of the East is that one's state of being is far more significant than the psychic feats it makes possible. And for us to recognize, value, and cultivate states conducive to psi seemingly requires us to be far more receptive than our Western approach to reality leads us to be.

The biblical admonition "Lest ye see miracles ye will not believe" underscores both the significance of supernormal powers and their drawback in spiritual traditions. While the contemplative life may lead one to undergo a psychospiritual change that includes the capability for psychic feats, another attribute of that same change dictates against their display: the truly holy man is also humble. This has been emphasized in the Christian tradition where, while saints are revered and known by their miracles, it is more basic qualities that are seen as more telling. C. H. Waddell writes of the fourth-century Desert Fathers:

> Of the depth of their spiritual experience they had little to say: but their every action showed a standard of values that turns the world upside down. It was their humility, their gentleness, their heart-breaking courtesy that was the seal of their sanctity to their contemporaries, far beyond abstinence or miracles or sign.

The ultimate meaning and lesson of meditation-related psychic phenomena may not be very different for us today: they stand as a signpost to a mode of being that transcends the normal limitations of ego.

Research on Meditation

Victor F. Emerson

VICTOR F. EMERSON *is presently a graduate student in psychology at Queen's University in Kingston, Ontario. His areas of interest in psychology are visual perception and meditative states.*

THE SCIENCE OF PSYCHOLOGY is about to complete a full circle. The introspection that flourished around the turn of the century was contested by the behaviorists, who overreacted by denying any "consciousness" to the particular animal under study. As a result, a trend toward a controlled introspection and subjectivism is now in progress, and one area, hitherto taboo, but now being investigated by legions of psychologists and physiologists, is meditation. In this paper the major studies of meditation will be reviewed and their methodology and findings analyzed. It will be seen that one of the more interesting indications of these studies is that the internal states of subjects during medita-

Reprinted from *The R. M. Bucke Memorial Society Newsletter-Review* 5, nos. 1 and 2 (Spring 1972) by permission of the author and the R. M. Bucke Memorial Society, 4453 Maisonneuve Blvd. West, Montreal, 215, Canada.

tion seem to be determined by the underlying religious philosophy that is used in meditation; a brief comment will also be given concerning the various measures taken and the means of interpreting them.

Generally speaking, the religious philosophies dealt with here can be divided in two: Zen Buddhism and the various schools of yoga in Hinduism. These will be briefly considered in turn.

Zen Buddhism is probably the most radical school of Buddhism. Basically, it teaches that the student must reach enlightenment[1] (which liberates him from the rebirth cycle) by scrupulously following a strict life style; his mode of thought is rapidly transformed to enable him to ask the appropriate questions of reality, and through meditation he gains the necessary insight to understand the answers. The object of this life style is to become increasingly aware of the environment while maintaining a passionless attitude toward external occurrences.

Yoga,[2] on the other hand, advocates withdrawal from the external world. Although there are minor philosophical differences between sects, the basic teaching is that to achieve liberation (*moksha*) from the wheel of rebirth (*samsara*) one must come to understand the essential unity of all things, including oneself, in Brahman, the all-pervading spirit of the universe. To accomplish this, one must detach oneself from the external world and turn inward to evade the distractions (*maya*) of objects, object-subject dichot-

---

[1] Enlightenment is variously termed *kan, kensho, satori,* or nirvana depending on the particular state referred to as well as the sect and its geographical location.

[2] When the term *yoga* pertains to the philosophical system, it is capitalized; when it refers to the physical discipline, the lowercase *y* is used.

omies, and even consciousness and thought. Turning inward implies far more than self-contemplation; it implies Self-contemplation, the realization of the self-Self (*atman-Atman*) and Self-Self (*Atman-Brahman*) identities. Personal feelings have no place in this scheme, and so yogic meditation is generally devoted to clearing the mind and consciousness and striving to achieve a state (or experience) called *samadhi* (higher meditation), the closest a living being can come to liberation. This is the technique of raja (royal) yoga, but other sects differ somewhat. For example, kriya (from the root *kr-*, to do) yoga, a popular form in Bengal, uses visualization of a god or other spiritual essence as an object of meditation (thus the term *kriya*; the disciple must produce an image), and the yogi interacts with this vision to achieve *samadhi*. This is the technique employed by the subjects tested by Das and Gastaut (1957).[3] Hatha yoga, a form common in the West, is the least spiritual of all, for it implies no super-sentient being or religion to assist the yogi in his meditative efforts; it is roughly this form of yoga that is investigated in studies performed on Westerners.

Until the advent of machines capable of recording man's internal goings-on, the rather outrageous claims surrounding yoga especially were nonverifiable. There were numerous claims of yogis who, in effect, entered a state of suspended animation during meditation, exhibiting slowing or stopping of the heart and respira-

---

[3] Allison (1970) describes an ingenious method of measuring respiration rate which has the advantage that, unlike other methods, it does not interfere with the meditator by trapping "dead" air. This involves suspending thermistors from a headband to points near the mouth and nostrils and translating the temperature fluctuations into respirations.

tion, insensitivity to external stimuli, etc., and these statements were generally dismissed by scientists as ludicrous and exploited by the gullible as demonstrating the existence of God (in whatever form they wished). Finally a handful of brave souls challenged the contemporary "scientific" attitude and prevailing conditions and used the technology available at that time to lend some rationality to the knowledge of the nature of those phenomena.

As many authors have mentioned (e.g., Bagchi and Wenger, 1957; Das and Gastaut, 1957), the greatest difficulty in conducting a study of this type is locating an experienced yogi who has no objection to being wired and taped for recording purposes. One must usually travel to India, weed through the mercenaries and charlatans who offer themselves as subjects, and then enlist the assistance of a true yogi. The latter step is undoubtedly the most difficult, since implicit in the yoga teaching is that one not flaunt the spiritual powers one acquires on the path to liberation. To evaluate the physiological manifestations of religious meditation, one must rigidly control the nature of the subjects as well as their sect, meditation posture, degree of practice, and age, for all these factors may affect the interpretation of the results. As will be seen, these controls are very rarely observed, and what has generally resulted in a mishmash of unintelligible results which, when translated across studies, states only that meditation is identical with neither sleep nor wakefulness. No valid conclusions concerning religious philosophy, amount of practice, etc., can be drawn from the majority of studies. The results from any one study may or may not be valid, depending on the nature of the controls used, if any. The studies that have employed the best methodology will be discussed below, and it will be seen that when there is some interstudy consistency in controls, much more information can be gained than when the controls are dissimilar.

Basically, the tools involved in measuring the internal states of meditators are electrocardiographs (EKG) for measuring heart rate, spirometers for measuring respiratory rate and ventilation, electromyographs (EMG) for recording muscle tone and muscle activity, and electroencephalographs (EEG) for recording brain wave pattern. Except for the latter, these are all relatively straightforward. The EEG, however, deserves some explaining, particularly since it is this measure that is of most interest in this review.

Most people are familiar with the basic pattern of an EEG tracing—a squiggly line that looks like a piece of wet spaghetti that was stretched and suddenly released. This tracing is usually taken to represent the electrical potential difference between any two points on the cortex. This record is often considered a macroanalysis of the activity of that area of the cortex being investigated—that is, the area beneath the two electrodes. The record is presumed to represent the summed activity of millions of cells and cannot be considered representative of any one cell; for that, other, more complex techniques, such as single-cell recording, are available. Such techniques can elucidate the role of smaller areas of the brain in various behavioral tasks. For the purpose of classifying general states of consciousness, however, one probably should consider the over-all activity of the cortex, and so the gross EEG is used.[4] Since the cortical electrical activity is translated onto a two-dimensional graph, two

[4] There are EEG oddities observed in sleep that will not be considered in this paper. The reader should keep in mind that it is possible that meditation states may produce similar physiological records to those obtained from sleep states and yet be a quite different state. This possibility will not be explored here.

direct measures may be made from the tracing: the amplitude (vertical axis) and the frequency, which is read from blocks of time (horizontal axis) and indicates the cyclical activity of the firing pattern. For convenience, and in correlation with behavioral observation, the brain wave patterns have been classified on the basis of their frequency into four types—beta, alpha, theta, and delta waves—which are in turn classed on a continuum according to amplitude. Beta waves are defined as the range above 14 hertz (hz), or cycles per second, and are indicative of a state of arousal. Alpha waves occur from 8–13 hz and indicate a state of relaxed wakefulness; they are generally observed in the majority of the population when the eyes are closed and the attention is not focused. Theta waves are 4–7 hz, indicating even lower arousal, and delta waves (below 3.5 hz) are usually observed only in sleep or coma. When the EEG is flat (no electrical activity in the cortex), the organism is considered dead.

A standard pattern is observed with these recordings; for example, a normal person generating alpha waves as he relaxes in his rocker will demonstrate a phenomenon known as *alpha block* if a disturbing event occurs in the environment—for example, if someone drops a glass in the kitchen. Alpha block is an abrupt cessation of (typically) high-amplitude alpha waves and the onset of low-amplitude beta waves. This is also known as desyncronization, since the cortical cells are no longer firing in synchrony (which is assumed to determine amplitude, all else being equal). What has occurred psychologically is that the stimulus (in this case a crash) has been received by the ear, which sent the message to the auditory cortex and the reticular activating system (RAS), a diffuse structure in the brain stem which regulates the level of arousal.

The abrupt onset of the stimulus caused the RAS to "alert" the rest of the brain to the presence of the stimulus generator, in a sense to prime the brain to respond to the stimulus. The RAS is directly responsible for the desynchronization of the EEG and the accompanying somersault of the person in the rocker. The various states of arousal are important in the survival of all animals, for it is the arousal level that will, to a large degree, determine the actions an intact animal will perform. For example, if an animal becomes aroused at the sound of a twig cracking nearby, it has the chance to flee from a predator, whereas if no arousal ensued, escape would be impossible. Similarly, if the animal became so aroused that it was confused, its chances of successful escape would be reduced. Thus, there is an "optimal" level of arousal for each situation. A corollary to alpha block exists, and that is that if a stimulus is repeatedly presented with no accompanying event of biological significance, the stimulus loses its importance to the organism and habituation of alpha blocks occurs, so that the alpha rhythm will persist uninterrupted through all sorts of clatter, such as when one settles into a rocker with jackhammers and automobile horns blaring outside the window.

Before examining the results of various studies, a few of the more common meditation postures will be described. This aspect of meditation has far too often been ignored, and it is to the credit of those authors who controlled for this factor or at least mentioned their subjects' postures that they did so, for, as will be shown below, the physiological conditions existing during meditation are often similar to the basal metabolic condition, and one must be careful not to mar the results by lumping data from a wide range of physiological states. This would occur if one were to classify the subjects meditating in different positions as one group; Ikegami (1970) has shown that for various Zen postures the activity levels of some muscles are different from posture to posture. Because of this, the metabolic rates of these muscles differ, and so the metabolism of the meditator varies. Considering such varied data as similar conceals the possible effects of posture on the various metabolic measures. Controls for this and other variables (e.g., age and length of practice) should be used whenever a variable may differentially influence metabolic rate. Since clinical researchers take great pains to insure interpatient uniformity when measuring basal metabolic rate, it is surprising to observe that few experimenters in the field have followed suit.

The various yoga postures are too numerous to mention, and the reader is advised to examine one of the many books on hatha yoga for a review of the standard postures. The one posture most frequently assumed for meditation is the full lotus posture, in which one sits cross-legged, with the soles of the feet facing upward while the feet rest on the thigh near the crotch. The spine is made as nearly vertical as possible, and the arms are extended so that the hands rest on the knees. The head is held rigidly vertical, with the gaze (through half-opened eyes) lowered.

There are also various Zen postures, most of which are not relevant to this discussion. The reader is referred to Ikegami (1970) for an excellent review of some postures and their metabolic costs. He showed that for the positions and muscles studied, Zen priests show less "internal fidgeting" (measured in terms of change of center of gravity) than laymen—specifically, markedly less (one-third to one-half) muscle activity.

Indeed, this is possibly the most striking thing about meditation; many authors have reported absolute silence from the EMG in the case of both yogis (e.g., Das and Gastaut, 1957) and Zen priests. The difference between Zen priests and laymen was greatest in the *kekkafuza* position, which is similar to the yoga full lotus posture except that the buttocks are rested on a cushion and the hands are folded in the lap. *Hankafuza* is identical to *kekkafuza* except that only one foot is placed on the contralateral thigh, the other foot being tucked underneath its opposite thigh; this posture was found to be the most restful posture for novices when maintained for thirty minutes. Alternative postures are *agura* (same as *kekkafuza*, but without the cushion) and *seiza*, in which the buttocks are rested on the heels, each calf folded under the ipsilateral thigh, and the knees either together or apart. Ikegami also noted that, in general, these postures can be maintained with increasing stability with age and practice, and he suggests that these, plus one's mental attitude, are salient factors in Zen meditation. A brief attempt at forming each of the postures should convince the reader of the necessity of controlling for these factors.

Empirically, the most interesting finding from the meditation studies is that meditators can demonstrate remarkable control of their brain wave patterns. By now it has become common knowledge that when people sit down to meditate, they produce copious quantities of alpha waves, and, unfortunately, one need not venture far to encounter one of the seemingly numberless advertisements for alpha-feedback machines, which (allegedly) remarkably enable one to learn in a matter of minutes to generate alpha waves and experience hitherto unknown bliss. Mulholland (1971) has delivered an inspired retort to this entire industry and its implications. He eloquently and bluntly suggests that the reason many Westerners "experience" a sense of transcendence during meditation is that they have never before taken the time to relax and discover their inner thoughts. His paper is an excellent critique of the methodology used in research on alpha conditioning and is somewhat applicable to some of the studies mentioned here. It is important that the reader realize that there is nothing magical about alpha waves; they are only indicative of an attentional state and appear spontaneously in the great majority of the population. Rather, what is important is the abnormalities observed in the brain wave patterns of the meditators, and it is these that will now be considered. It will be seen that the results of different studies seem to indicate that the religion of the meditator determines to a great extent the way in which his EEG pattern as well as his metabolism will change during the course of meditation.

Bagchi and Wenger (1957) appear to have been the first to note that some yogis, who when meditating are producing the basic resting EEG pattern (alpha waves), exhibit no response to an external stimulus (noise, in particular), whereas an alpha block would be expected. Similarly, there is no change in the galvanic skin response (GSR; a marked decrease in skin resistance indicates emotionality) in this condition. The EEG observation, which was objectively recorded in only one subject, was supported by the negative verbal reports of two other subjects. That the subject was not sleeping was established by inspection of the EEG record.

Anand, Chhina, and Singh (1961 *a*) subjected two yogis to external stimulation both before and during meditation. The stimuli consisted of turning on a strong light, banging on an object, vibrating a tuning fork, and touching the yogis with a hot glass tube. Before meditation, both yogis showed persistent alpha block. During meditation, however, no alpha block was observed. Similarly, two other yogis, who claimed to have developed high pain thresholds, were able to keep one hand in 4° C. water for 45–55 minutes with no EEG disturbance or apparent discomfort. This paradigm has been criticized by Barber (1970) for not including the appropriate control groups, but it is the opinion of this author that, for the pre- and during-meditation stimulation study, adequate controls were observed, and these results can be interpreted as supporting the finding of Bagchi and Wenger (1957). From these studies it appears that some yogis have succeeded in training their bodies to function according to their religious beliefs during meditation.

On the other hand, there are greatly differing results in the studies on Zen meditation. Kasamatsu and Hirai (1966) showed that Zen masters produced continuous alpha waves that were interrupted by a click stimulus. In these subjects, alpha blocks habituation did not obtain after repeated presentations of the stimulus, whereas control subjects did exhibit habituation. These authors, in a carefully controlled study, also demonstrated progressive EEG changes with increasing Zen practice; those subjects with 0–5 years of experience, for example, showed no rhythmical theta waves, whereas these waves appeared regularly in some subjects with 21–40 years of experience. They conclude that the EEG changes correlate highly with the subjects' proficiency and degree of training in Zen.

As well, Akishige (1970) reports that Kasamatsu, Hirai, and Izawa (1963) also found no habituation of Zen subjects to a click stimulus, whereas controls habituated around the tenth presentation. Furthermore, Kasamatsu and Hirai (1966) note that the blocking time was short and that the alpha waves returned quite soon after the stimulus. These results suggest that the meditators were in a markedly different state from the yogis in the studies cited above; however, this suggestion is readily, albeit tentatively, explained. As was noted earlier, the underlying philosophies of these two sects are quite different; the yogi abandons the external world, turning his attention inward, whereas the Zen devotee maintains a passionless involvement in the environment. The EEG results, when examined in this light, suggest, as Tart (1969) and Barber (1970) have observed, that these results cannot meaningfully be grouped under one label. One must avoid making noncommittal mumbo jumbo statements about *the* "meditation state" and classify the results of the studies according to various factors; in this instance, religious philosophy appears to be particularly relevant, although with such small numbers of subjects and such few studies this suggestion can only be tentative. In all these studies, however, the subjects (with appropriate controls) meditated (presumably in approximately the same position, since full lotus and either *hankafuza* or *kekkafuza* are the preferred positions) and during meditation were exposed to roughly similar auditory stimuli. In one case (the yogis) no EEG change was noted, whereas in the other (Zen priests), persistent alpha block obtained.

Das and Gastaut (1957), studying subjects practicing kriya yoga, found strikingly different results. Rather than observing persistent alpha rhythms, which the majority of researchers have noted in studies on other sects, these authors found extremely fast beta activity (indicative of high arousal) with high amplitude waves (frequency up to 40 hz, amplitude 30–50 microvolts) which were paralleled in their gradual development by an acceleration of the heart rhythm. In addition, they note that various stimuli applied during meditation had absolutely no effect on the EEG. This latter finding is again strong evidence of withdrawal from the environment, and once again the philosophy of the sect explains the EEG results. Rather than pursuing an "objectless" meditation, as were the yogis studied by Anand et al. (1961 *a*), the disciples of kriya yoga were focusing their attention on visions and were actively involved in summoning the *kundalini* (spirit energy). As their meditation progressed, this energy was purported to have traveled from its resting place at the base of the spine up the spinal column until it reached the peak of the head, at which time ecstasy occurred. This voyage was accompanied by an unfolding vision that served to inform the yogi of the locus of the *kundalini* and thus serve as an "autofeedback" mechanism. The EEG changes seemed to parallel this as well.

These few studies constitute the greater portion of the EEG work on authentic yogis and Zen priests. It cannot be stressed enough that this collection is far too inadequate for the appreciation of the finer effects of meditation, and much further work is needed. There are great methodological differences among these studies, and any hypothesis alleging to show inter-sect differences must also take into account the low signal-to-noise ratio produced by the use of varied methodologies. The hypothesis advanced above that EEG changes follow the course charted by religious philosophy is readily testable, and future data on this point should be interesting. Again, however, caution must be advised, for the necessary control groups, sampling procedures, and classification of results are absolutely indispensable if one hopes to make meaningful statements about the data.

Various other studies have been conducted on meditation of nonreligious subjects. Most notable among these are the recent studies by Wallace and co-workers (Wallace, 1970; Wallace, Benson, and Wilson, 1971; Wallace and Benson, 1972) in which physiological measures were recorded from students of Transcendental Meditation as taught by the Maharishi Mahesh Yogi. Physiologically these results are most interesting, and in general support the findings obtained by other researchers in studies on true yogis and Zen priests: decreased oxygen consumption and carbon dioxide elimination (in accord with the study by Anand et al. [1961 *b*] of a yogi sealed in an airtight box); slightly decreased respiration rate (other researchers, e.g., Akishige [1970], Allison [1970], Bagchi and Wenger [1957], Brosse [1946], and Miles [1964], have reported a marked decrease in respiration in various types of subjects, sometimes as low as 40–50 per cent of "basal" need); a decrease in blood lactate; and a rapid rise in skin resistance (Bagchi and Wenger, 1957). As well, persistent alpha activity in the EEG was observed. All these signs are consistent with the existence of a remarkable state of relaxation, which is the goal of this form of meditation. But it must be emphasized that this work cannot justifiably be equated with the studies on religious meditators, for the Maharishi Mahesh Yogi's version of Transcendental Meditation has no underlying religious philosophy. Consequently, one cannot infer that the subjects have the same motivation within and across studies. Comparisons can be made casually (as above)—for example to observe the effects of sitting down and relaxing—but we have seen indications that beyond this point there are subtleties of religious meditation that have physiological effects extending far beyond those observed in Wallace's subjects. In addition, there is the complicating factor that the subjects used by Wallace and his co-workers were from a vastly different subject population from those tested in India and Japan. Also, the American subjects were lumped regardless of degree of proficiency, length of practice, etc., a process that may or may not affect the over-all interpretation of the results but that certainly obscures finer trends. To be sure, many of the Asian studies are guilty of the same transgressions, although these studies are usually more descriptive of their subjects. A further confounding factor has been the American practice of instructing the subject when to begin and finish meditating, a procedure that would be unthinkable in a religious setting.

These discrepancies should not detract from the implication of this work, however. In the majority of cases, what is happening is that the meditators are producing what Wallace et al. (1971) have labeled a "wakeful hypometabolic" state. In many cases, an approximation to this state has been produced in a biofeedback paradigm using alpha waves as the pertinent measure. Much similar work has been done with feedback to produce alterations in heart rate and blood pressure. However, the religious studies have demonstrated that many people, specifically yogis, are capable of this type of autonomic conditioning with no apparent feedback. The work of Brosse (1946, 1950) and Bagchi and Wenger (1957) demonstrates this learning of cardiac control. Other studies, many of which have been mentioned above (e.g., Allison, 1970; Bagchi and Wenger, 1957) attest to superb respiratory control which is undoubtedly due to the importance of breathing exercises in all forms of meditation.

Aside from the obvious clinical implications, these practices warrant consideration from the standpoint of emergency training, as Miles (1964) has suggested. For example, if special meditational breathing practices were mandatory in a miner-training program, how many lives could be saved when cave-ins cut off air supplies? It has been repeatedly shown that meditation lowers the metabolic rate to the vicinity of the basal rate or even, in some instances, below it (Akishige, 1970; Anand et al., 1961 *b*), which would serve to prolong life where vital elements are restricted. Instead of panicking in such situations, it is obviously more beneficial to relax (contrary to "instinctive" reactions);[5] however, it is also important not to fall asleep, for O_2 consumption has been shown to be much higher in sleep than in meditation (Wallace and Benson, 1972).

In a similar vein, cardiac control exercises may be helpful in warding off heart disease. No data bearing directly on this question have been produced, to the author's knowledge, but Brosse (1946, 1950) has shown that subjects can regulate cardiac arrhythmia, and various studies on yogis have demonstrated that control of the heart is possible.

Furthermore, Miller (1969) in his classic study of autonomic conditioning in chemically paralyzed rats has shown that these animals can be taught to perform some rather remarkable feats, such as controlling intestinal motility, heart rate, and even blood flow in

[5] I am indebted to Dr. P. H. Platenius for bringing this aspect of meditation to my attention as well as for generally assisting me in my approach to meditation states. His helpful comments on the manuscript are also appreciated.

one ear (while not affecting the other). The latter finding, if it could be produced in nonimmobilized humans,[6] may have implications in the control of cancer; if a patient could be taught to reduce the blood flow to the tumor, the progress of the cancer could possibly be retarded or even stopped.

Of course, much research must precede any implementation of such therapies. To ensure that the experimental results are valid and not artifactual, proper research methodology in this area must be developed and rigorously observed. The breakthrough in autonomic conditioning is not to be underestimated, for it has effectively returned the "involuntary" half of man's body to his control, and despite the ominous implications for behaviorism and standard therapeutic techniques, it should be expected that medicine and psychotherapy, as well as psychology and physiology, will greatly benefit from accepting and developing this phenomenon.

It is to be hoped that future research will take into account those variables that have been neglected in previous studies and that may be particularly relevant in assessing the metabolic effects of meditation. In particular, controls should be established for such factors as posture, age, and length of practice of the subjects. In addition, if subjects are classified according to religious philosophy, perhaps the "effect" of this "variable," if any, can be properly evaluated.

[6] This is a big if, but evidence suggests that it is not so unreasonable. For related work, the reader is referred to Sargent, Green, and Walters (1971) for thermoregulation of the hands in the treatment of migraine and to Wenger and Bagchi (1961) for a report of voluntary forehead perspiration by a yogi.

REFERENCES

Akishige, Y. "A Historical Survey of the Psychological Studies on Zen." In *Psychological Studies on Zen*, edited by Y. Akishige. *Bulletin of the Faculty of Literature of Kyushu University*, no. 2 (V), Fukuoka, 1970.

Allison, J. "Respiratory Changes during Transcendental Meditation." *Lancet*, no. 7651 (April 18, 1970).

Anand, B. K., Chhina, G. S., and Singh, B. "Some Aspects of Electroencephalographic Studies in Yogis." *Electroencephalography and Clinical Neurophysiology* 13 (1961): 452–56 (*a*).

——. "Studies on Shri Ramanand Yogi during His Stay in an Air-tight Box." *Indian Journal of Medical Research* 49 (1961): 82–89 (*b*).

Bagchi, B. L., and Wenger, M. A. "Electro-physiological Correlates of Some Yogi Exercises." In *First International Congress of Neurological Sciences*, III, edited by L. van Bogaert and J. Radermecker. New York: Pergamon Press, 1957.

Barber, T. X. *LSD, Marihuana, Yoga and Hypnosis*. Chicago: Aldine Publishing Company, 1970.

Brosse, T. "Altruism and Creativity as Biological Factors of Human Evolution." In *Explorations in Altruistic Love and Behavior*, edited by P. A. Sorokin. Boston: Beacon Press, 1950.

——. "A Psycho-physiological Study. *Main Currents in Modern Thought* 4 (1946): 77–84.

Das, N. N., and Gastaut, H. "Variations de l'activité électrique du cerveau, du coeur, et des muscles squelettiques au cours de la méditation et de l'extase yogique." *Electroencephalography and Clinical Neurophysiology*, 1957, supp. 6, 211–19.

Ikegami, R. "Psychological Study of Zen Posture." In *Psychological Studies on Zen*, edited by Y. Akishige. *Bulletin of the Faculty of Literature of Kyushu University*, no. 2 (V), Fukuoka, 1970.

Kasamatsu, A., and Hirai, T. "An Electroencephalographic Study on the Zen Meditation (Zazen)." *Folio Psychiatrica et Neurologica Japonica* 20 (1966): 315–36. (Reprinted in *Altered States of Consciousness*, edited by C. T. Tart. New York: John Wiley & Sons, 1969.)

Kasamatsu, A., Hirai, T., and Izawa, H. "Medical and Psychological Studies on Zen." *Proceedings of the Twenty-seventh Convention of the Japanese Psychological Association*, 1963, p. 347. (Cited by Akishige, 1970.)

Miles, W. R. "Oxygen Consumption during Three Yoga-Type Breathing Patterns." *Journal of Applied Physiology* 19 (1964): 75–82.

Miller, N. E. "Learning of Visceral and Glandular Responses." *Science* 163 (1969): 434–45.

Mulholland, T. "Can You Really Turn On with Alpha?" Paper presented at the meeting of the Massachusetts Psychological Association, 1971.

Sargent, J. D., Green, E. E., and Walters, E. D. "Preliminary Report on the Use of Autogenic Feedback Techniques in the Treatment of Migraine and Tension Headaches." Unpublished manuscript, 1971.

Tart, C. T. "The Psychophysiology of Some Altered States of Consciousness." In *Altered States of Consciousness*, edited by C. T. Tart. New York: John Wiley & Sons, 1969.

Wallace, R. K. "Physiological Effects of Transcendental Meditation." *Science* 167 (1970): 1751–54.

Wallace, R. K., and Benson, H. "The Physiology of Meditation." *Scientific American* 226, no. 2 (February, 1972): 84–90.

Wallace, R. K., Benson, H., and Wilson, A. F. "A Wakeful Hypometabolic Physiologic State." *American Journal of Physiology* 221, no. 3 (1971): 795–99.

Wenger, M. A., and Bagchi, B. K. "Studies of Autonomic Functions in Practitioners of Yoga in India." *Behavioral Science* 6 (1961): 312–23.

Postscript: A Little More Effort

Shri Mata Ji

SHRI MATA JI is the mother of Satguru Maharaj Ji, who is the spiritual leader of the Divine Light Mission. This discourse was given in May 1972 at the mission's headquarters in Concord, Massachusetts.

THERE WAS ONCE A YOGI who lived a very strict life in the forest, living on berries and having no possessions of his own. He was just sitting there, hoping to find God. Forty years passed and still he was sitting there, but still God didn't come. You see, there is a way to do everything, and this yogi didn't know the way to find God. And so God didn't come. The yogi had let his hair grow very long, and his fingernails too, and he had smeared himself all over with ashes and he looked like nothing on earth. He had almost lost consciousness of his body altogether.

Finally he became tired of that way of life because the birds used to come and nest in his hair year after year because that was all he was good for. He was a fine place for birds to bring up their children. So finally he got bored of just sitting around and said to himself, "This is no good. I'm going back, and I'm going to get married. Even if I can't see God, at least I can enjoy bringing up some children of my own."

He was on his way back from the forest to live in the world when he ran across a famous dancer who was rather short of money. She said that she was going to dance in the palace of the king in a nearby town, although people told her that the king was a miser who wouldn't give her a penny. She told the yogi that she was sure he would give her something if she danced well enough and long enough.

So the yogi, the sadhu, thought that this would be a splendid way to be introduced to worldly life: he would go to court and watch this famous dancer dance before a king. And he went to the palace and he sat there in the corner with his long hair and his blanket. And the king was there and his son and daughter. And the dancer danced, and she danced, and she danced.

She danced until the first light of dawn crept into the courtyard, but still the king threw her no gold coin, tossed her no purse, and at last she became tired of waiting and sang to her husband:

> We won't grow rich by standing here.
> I think we'd best be gone, my dear.

But her husband, who was playing the tabla, sang back to her:

> We've done so much.
> There's not much more to do.
> Let's not stop here.
> Let's see this business through.

Now, this yogi was a naked yogi and his blanket was the only cover he had. But he was so overwhelmed by this verse that the husband sang that he forgot all about his nakedness and took his blanket and threw it across to the dancer. And the king's daughter threw her diamond earrings across to the woman, and the king's son took off his ring and threw that.

The dancer was very satisfied, more than satisfied, by this unexpected turn of events. But the king was very angry about it. And his reason was this: In that part of the world it was the custom that the richest man present would be the first to give a gift. So the king was very angry, and he asked the sadhu, "Why did you do that? Why did you give her your blanket before I had made my contribution?" And the sadhu, the yogi, said, "O King, I had nothing else to give her, so I gave her my blanket. If I were the emperor, I would have given her all my lands, my palaces and slaves, because she and her husband just saved my life. When her husband sang, 'We've done so much. There's not much more to do. Let's not stop here. Let's see this business through,' I suddenly realized that God was giving me one last chance. I have been meditating and trying to see God for forty years, but recently my mind has been beginning to trick me. It has been persuading me to give up my attempt to see God and to go back into the world and get married instead. But when I heard that verse, I understood something. I saw that if I made a little more effort, my whole lifetime's search would be rewarded. But if I gave up now, I would have wasted my whole life. So I was simply overwhelmed that they should give me such good advice, especially as they didn't even intend it for me; and I gave them my blanket because that was all I had to give them in return."

So the king turned to his daughter and asked her why she had given her diamonds to the dancer, and she replied, "O Father, what can I say? I was just going to commit a terrible sin. Every time I have asked you to arrange a marriage for me, you have said, 'Okay, I will arrange it soon.' But you were so stingy that it never occurred to you that I was slowly growing old and you never did anything about it. So I finally got very impatient and tonight I was going to run away with the Grand Minister's son. But when I heard that verse the dancer's husband sang, I realized that if I had managed to wait this long, I might as well be patient a little longer. And when I saw that that little ditty had saved the reputation of our whole family, I just gave them my earrings. It was the least I could do."

And then the king turned to his son and asked him why he had given away his ring. And the son replied, "Tonight would have been the last night of your life if it weren't for the dancer and her husband. Recently I have become completely fed up with your miserly ways. You refuse to marry my sister, although she keeps asking you to find her a husband, and you are completely reluctant to allow me any power, although I am your son and heir and a grown man. Tonight I was going to kill you, and then I would have given my sister's hand to a worthy husband and ruled the kingdom to the best of my ability because everyone was getting completely tired of you and your hesitations. But when I heard that verse, I said to myself, 'I have waited this long. Perhaps I should be patient a little longer.' So that poem saved you from death at the hands of your son; it saved me from killing my own father; and it saved our land from the rule of a murderer. That little ditty worked wonders for us all. And that's why I gave my ring to the pair of them."

At this point, it dawned on the king that something

marvelous had happened. He appointed his son to rule his kingdom, married his daughter off to a brave and gentle prince from a neighboring state, sent lavish presents to the dancer and her husband, and then went off himself with the yogi in search of God. And all because of a little poem that said, "Let's not stop here. Let's see this business through."

So this is the point that I'm trying to get across, dear people: Have a little patience, practice this meditation, and you will all live happily ever after.

Appendix: Useful Guides

BOOKS

Altered States of Consciousness. Charles Tart, ed. Garden City, N.Y.: Anchor, 1972.

Approaches to Meditation. Virginia Hanson, ed. Wheaton, Ill.: Quest, 1973.

Concentration: An Approach to Meditation. Ernest Wood. Wheaton, Ill.: Quest, 1949.

Concentration and Meditation. Christmas Humphries. Baltimore: Penguin, 1968.

Creative Intelligence through Transcendental Meditation. Harold Bloomfield, Michael Cain, and Dennis Jaffe. New York: Delacorte, 1974.

Explorations in Awareness. John W. Aiken. Socorro, N.M.: Church of the Awakening, 1966.

The Heart of Buddhist Meditation. Nyanaponika Thera. New York: Samuel Weiser, 1962.

The Highest State of Consciousness. John White, ed. Garden City, N.Y.: Anchor, 1972.

How to Enter the Silence. H. Rhodes Wallace. London: Fowler & Co., 1968.

How to Meditate. Sebastian Temple. Chicago: Radial Press, 1971.

Introduction to Contemplative Meditation. M. V. Dunlop. London: Billing & Sons, 1929.

Meditation. Adelaide Gardner. Wheaton, Ill.: Quest, 1968.

Meditation: Gateway to Light. Elsie Sechrist. Virginia Beach, Va.: Association for Research and Enlightenment, 1964.

Meditation in the Silence. E. V. Ingraham. Lee's Summit, Mo.: Unity, 1969.

Meditation: The Inward Art. Bradford Smith. Philadelphia: Lippincott, 1962.

Metaphysical Meditation. Paramahansa Yogananda. Los Angeles: Self Realization Fellowship, 1964.

Philosophy of Meditation. Haridas Chaudhuri. New York: Philosophical Library, 1965.

The Practice of Meditation. Charles Bowness. New York: Samuel Weiser, 1971.

Psycho-Yoga: The Practice of Mind Control. B. Edwin. New York: Citadel, 1967.

The Secrets of Chinese Meditation. Charles Luk. New York: Samuel Weiser, 1971.

The Silent Path. Michel J. Eastcott. New York: Samuel Weiser, 1969.

Spiritual Community Guide. Spiritual Community, Box 1080, San Rafael, Calif. 1972. (Tells where meditation instruction can be obtained.)

Ten Ways to Meditate. Paul Reps. New York: Walker/Weatherhill, 1969.

The Three Pillars of Zen. Philip Kapleau, ed. Boston: Beacon, 1965.

Tranquility without Pills. Jhan Robbins and David Fisher. New York: Wyden, 1972.

Why and How of Meditation. Russ Michael. Lakemont, Ga.: CSA Press, 1971.

The Well and the Cathedral: A Cycle of Process Meditation. Ira Progoff. New York: Dialogue House Library, 1971.

Year One Catalog. Ira Friedlander. New York: Harper & Row, 1972. (Tells where meditation instruction can be obtained.)

RECORDINGS

Association for Research and Enlightenment
Box 595
Virginia Beach, Va. 23451
("Introduction to Meditation," by H. B. Puryear)

Big Sur Recordings
117 Mitchell Blvd.
San Rafael, Calif. 94903

MEA
Box 303
Sausalito, Calif. 94965
(Many tapes by Alan Watts)

Noumedia Co.
Box 750
Port Chester, N.Y. 10573
(Tapes on Ram Dass, Sufism, Zen Buddhism)

Dr. William R. Parker
1807 Westcliff Dr.
Newport Beach, Calif. 92660
("Relaxation/Meditation"—a Christian meditation)

Spiritual Frontiers Fellowship
800 Custer Ave.
Evanston, Ill. 60202
("How to Meditate," by Arthur Ford)

Yasodhara Ashram
Kootenay Bay, Box 9
British Columbia, Canada
(LP records of guided meditation and mantras)

FILMS

Hartley Productions
Cat Rock Rd.
Cos Cob, Conn. 06807
(Films on yoga, Zen Buddhism, Tibetan Buddhism, Sufism)

MISCELLANEOUS

Esalen Institute
1793 Union St.
San Francisco, Calif. 94123
(The catalog, which costs $2, offers many opportunities for instruction in meditational techniques.)

Lucis Trust
Suite 566-7
866 United Nations Plaza
New York, N.Y. 10017
(Free meditation instruction on the premises)

Meditation Group for the New Age
Box 566
Ojai, Calif. 93023
(Free booklets by mail giving a home course in meditation)

University of the Trees
Box 644
Boulder Creek, Calif. 95006
(A three-year course in meditation led by Christopher Hills)

Students International Meditation Society (SIMS)
1015 Gayley Ave.
Los Angeles, Calif.
(National headquarters for Transcendental Meditation centers)